Congressional
Research Service
Informing the legislative debate since 1914 _____

Navy Littoral Combat Ship (LCS) Program: Background and Issues for Congress

Ronald O'Rourke

Specialist in Naval Affairs

June 4, 2014

Congressional Research Service

7-5700

www.crs.gov

RL33741

Summary

A total of 20 Littoral Combat Ships (LCSs) have been funded through FY2014. The Navy had been planning to procure an eventual total of 52 LCSs, but on February 24, 2014, Secretary of Defense Chuck Hagel announced that "no new contract negotiations beyond 32 ships will go forward" and that the Navy is to submit "alternative proposals to procure a capable and lethal small surface combatant, generally consistent with the capabilities of a frigate. I've directed the Navy to consider a completely new design, existing ship designs, and a modified LCS."

LCSs have been procured since FY2010 under a pair of 10-ship, fixed-price incentive (FPI) block buy contracts that the Navy awarded to the two LCS builders—Lockheed and Austal USA—on December 29, 2010. Under these contracts, which cover the years FY2010-FY2015, four LCSs (numbers 21 through 24) were to be requested for procurement in FY2015. The Navy's proposed FY2015 budget, however, requests funding for the procurement of three rather than four LCSs, suggesting that one of the two LCS block buy contracts will not be fully implemented in its final year.

The Navy's request for three rather than four LCSs in FY2015 and Hagel's February 24 announcement that "no new contract negotiations beyond 32 ships will go forward" and that the Navy is to submit "alternative proposals to procure a capable and lethal small surface combatant, generally consistent with the capabilities of a frigate" raise several potential oversight issues for Congress, including the Navy's plan for determining which of the two LCS builders would receive one LCS in FY2015 rather than two, and the analytical basis for the actions affecting the LCS program announced by Hagel on February 24.

The LCS is a relatively inexpensive Navy surface combatant equipped with modular "plug-and-fight" mission packages for countering mines, small boats, and diesel-electric submarines, particularly in littoral (i.e., near-shore) waters. Two very different LCS designs are being built. One was developed by an industry team led by Lockheed; the other was developed by an industry team that was led by General Dynamics. The Lockheed design is built at the Marinette Marine shipyard at Marinette, WI; the General Dynamics design is built at the Austal USA shipyard at Mobile, AL.

The LCS program has been controversial due to past cost growth, design and construction issues with the lead ships built to each design, concerns over the ships' survivability (i.e., ability to withstand battle damage), and concerns over whether the ships are sufficiently armed and would be able to perform their stated missions effectively. Prior to Secretary Hagel's February 24, 2014, announcement, some observers, citing one or more of these issues, had proposed truncating the LCS program. In response to criticisms of the LCS program, the Navy has acknowledged certain problems and stated that it was taking action to correct them, disputed other arguments made against the program, and (until Hagel's February 24, 2014, announcement) maintained its support for completing the planned program of 52 ships.

Contents

Figures

Tables

Appendixes

Contacts

Introduction

A total of 20 Littoral Combat Ships (LCSs) have been funded through FY2014. The Navy had been planning to procure an eventual total of 52 LCSs, but on February 24, 2014, Secretary of Defense Chuck Hagel announced that "no new contract negotiations beyond 32 ships will go forward" and that the Navy is to submit "alternative proposals to procure a capable and lethal small surface combatant, generally consistent with the capabilities of a frigate. I've directed the Navy to consider a completely new design, existing ship designs, and a modified LCS."[1]

LCSs have been procured since FY2010 under a pair of 10-ship, fixed-price incentive (FPI) block buy contracts that the Navy awarded to the two LCS builders—Lockheed and Austal USA—on December 29, 2010. Under these contracts, which cover the years FY2010-FY2015, four LCSs (numbers 21 through 24) were to be requested for procurement in FY2015. The Navy's proposed FY2015 budget, however, requests funding for the procurement of three rather than four LCSs, suggesting that one of the two LCS block buy contracts will not be fully implemented in its final year.

The Navy's request for three rather than four LCSs in FY2015 and Hagel's February 24 announcement that "no new contract negotiations beyond 32 ships will go forward" and that the Navy is to submit "alternative proposals to procure a capable and lethal small surface combatant, generally consistent with the capabilities of a frigate" raise several potential oversight issues for Congress, including the Navy's plan for determining which of the two LCS builders would receive one LCS in FY2015 rather than two, and the analytical basis for the actions affecting the LCS program announced by Hagel on February 24.

The issue for Congress is whether to approve, reject, or modify both the Navy's request to procure three LCSs (and also some LCS mission packages) in FY2015 and the actions affecting the LCS program announced by Hagel on February 24. Congress's decisions on the LCS program and the potential successor program will affect Navy capabilities and funding requirements, and the shipbuilding industrial base.

Background

The Program in General

The following sections describe the LCS program as it existed just prior to Hagel's February 24, 2014, announcement that that "no new contract negotiations beyond 32 ships will go forward" and that the Navy is to submit "alternative proposals to procure a capable and lethal small surface combatant, generally consistent with the capabilities of a frigate."

---

[1] DOD News Transcript, "Remarks by Secretary Hagel and Gen. Dempsey on the fiscal year 2015 budget preview in the Pentagon Briefing Room," February 24, 2014, accessed February 25, 2014, at http://www.defense.gov/transcripts/transcript.aspx?transcriptid=5377.

The LCS in Brief

The LCS program was announced on November 1, 2001.[2] The LCS is a relatively inexpensive Navy surface combatant that is to be equipped with modular "plug-and-fight" mission packages, including unmanned vehicles (UVs). Rather than being a multimission ship like the Navy's larger surface combatants, the LCS is to be a focused-mission ship, meaning a ship equipped to perform one primary mission at any given time. The ship's mission orientation can be changed by changing out its mission packages. The basic version of the LCS, without any mission packages, is referred to as the LCS sea frame.

The LCS's originally stated primary missions are antisubmarine warfare (ASW), mine countermeasures (MCM), and surface warfare (SUW) against small boats (including so-called "swarm boats"), particularly in littoral (i.e., near-shore) waters. The LCS program includes the development and procurement of ASW, MCM, and SUW mission packages for LCS sea frames. These three primary missions appear oriented toward countering, among other things, some of the littoral anti-access/area-denial (A2/AD) capabilities that have been fielded in recent years by Iran,[3] although they could also be used to counter similar A2/AD capabilities that might be fielded by other countries.

Additional potential missions for the LCS include peacetime engagement and partnership-building operations; intelligence, surveillance, and reconnaissance (ISR) operations; maritime security and intercept operations (including anti-piracy operations); support of Marines or special operations forces; and homeland defense operations. An LCS might perform these missions at any time, regardless of its installed mission module, although an installed mission module might enhance an LCS's ability to perform some of these missions.

The LCS displaces about 3,000 tons, making it about the size of a corvette (i.e., a light frigate) or a Coast Guard cutter. It has a maximum speed of more than 40 knots, compared to something more than 30 knots for the Navy cruisers and destroyers. The LCS has a shallower draft than Navy cruisers and destroyers, permitting it to operate in certain coastal waters and visit certain shallow-draft ports that are not accessible to Navy cruisers and destroyers.

Planned Procurement Quantities

Until February 24, 2014, the Navy had planned to procure 52 LCS sea frames.[4] A force of 52 LCSs would account for 17%, or about one-sixth, of the Navy's planned fleet of about 306 ships

---

[2] On November 1, 2001, the Navy announced that it was launching a Future Surface Combatant Program aimed at acquiring a family of next-generation surface combatants. This new family of surface combatants, the Navy stated, would include three new classes of ships: a destroyer called the DD(X)—later redesignated the DDG-1000—for the precision long-range strike and naval gunfire mission; a cruiser called the CG(X) for the air defense and ballistic missile mission, and a smaller combatant called the Littoral Combat Ship (LCS) to counter submarines, small surface attack craft, and mines in heavily contested littoral (near-shore) areas. The DDG-1000 was truncated to a total of three ships in 2009, and the CG(X) program was terminated in 2010. For more on the DDG-1000 program, see CRS Report RL32109, *Navy DDG-51 and DDG-1000 Destroyer Programs: Background and Issues for Congress*, by Ronald O'Rourke. For more on the CG(X) program, see CRS Report RL34179, *Navy CG(X) Cruiser Program: Background for Congress*, by Ronald O'Rourke.

[3] For a discussion of Iran's littoral A2/AD capabilities, including submarines, mines, and small boats, see CRS Report R42335, *Iran's Threat to the Strait of Hormuz*, coordinated by Kenneth Katzman.

[4] Until January 2013, the Navy had planned to procure a total of 55 LCS sea frames. A January 2013 Navy report to Congress adjusted some of the Navy's ship force-level objectives, including the objective for small surface (continued...)

of all types.[5] The Navy prior to February 24, 2014, had planned to procure 64 LCS mission packages (16 ASW, 24 MCM, and 24 SUW) for the 52 LCS sea frames. **Table 1** shows past (FY2005-FY2014) and projected (FY2014-FY2018) annual procurement quantities for LCS sea frames under the Navy's FY2015 budget submission.

Table 1. Past (FY2005-FY2014) and Projected (FY2015-FY2018) Annual LCS Sea Frame Procurement Quantities

(As shown in the Navy's FY2015 budget submission)

FY05	FY06	FY07	FY08	FY09	FY10	FY11
1	1	0	0	2	2	2
FY12	FY13	FY14	FY15	FY16	FY17	FY18
4	4	4	3	3	3	3

Source: Prepared by CRS based on FY2015 Navy budget submission.

Notes: (1) The two ships shown in FY2005 and FY2006 were funded through Navy's research and development account rather than the Navy's shipbuilding account. (2) The figures for FY2006-FY2008 do not include five LCSs (two in FY2006, two in FY2007, and one in FY2008) that were funded in those years but later canceled by the Navy. For details on these five canceled ships, see **Table B-1** in **Appendix B**. (3) Funding appropriated for the four LCSs procured in FY2013 was reduced by the March 1, 2013, sequester on FY2013 funding. (4) The Navy's FY2014 five-year (FY2014-FY2019) shipbuilding plan shows two additional ships in FY2019. These are, presumably, the first two ships in the proposed follow-on program for a ship "generally consistent with the capabilities of a frigate."

Two LCS Designs

On May 27, 2004, the Navy awarded contracts to two industry teams—one led by Lockheed Martin, the other by General Dynamics (GD)—to design two versions of the LCS, with options for each team to build up to two LCSs each. The LCS designs developed by the two teams are quite different—the Lockheed team's design is based on a steel semi-planing monohull (with an aluminum superstructure), while the GD team's design is based on an all-aluminum trimaran hull (see **Figure 1**). The two ships also use different built-in combat systems (i.e., different collections of built-in sensors, computers, software, and tactical displays) that were designed by each industry team. The Navy states that both LCS designs meet the Key Performance Parameters (KPPs) for the LCS program.

(...continued)

combatants—a category that in the future is to consist solely of LCSs—which was reduced from 55 ships to 52 ships. (Department of the Navy, *Report to Congress [on] Navy Combatant Vessel Force Structure Requirement*, January 2013, 3 pp. The cover letters for the report were dated January 31, 2013.)

[5] For more on the Navy's planned fleet, see CRS Report RL32665, *Navy Force Structure and Shipbuilding Plans: Background and Issues for Congress*, by Ronald O'Rourke.

Figure 1. Lockheed LCS Design (Top) and General Dynamics LCS Design (Bottom)

Source: U.S. Navy file photo accessed by CRS at http://www.navy.mil/list_all.asp?id=57917 on January 6, 2010.

Two LCS Shipyards

The Lockheed LCS design is built at the Marinette Marine shipyard at Marinette, WI.[6] The GD LCS design is built at the Austal USA shipyard at Mobile, AL.[7] Odd-numbered LCSs (i.e., LCS-1, LCS-3, LCS-5, and so on) use the Lockheed design; even-numbered LCSs (i.e., LCS-2, LCS-4, LCS-6, and so on) use the GD design.

LCSs in Service

LCS-1 entered service on November 8, 2008; LCS-2 entered service on January 16, 2010; LCS-3 entered service on August 6, 2012; and LCS-4 entered service on January 27, 2014.

Mission Package Deliveries Initial Operational Capability (IOC) Dates

Initial increments (i.e., versions) of LCS mission packages are undergoing testing. The Navy stated in its FY2015 budget submission that Increments I and II of the SUW mission package are scheduled to achieve IOC in the fourth quarter of FY2014, that Increment I of the MCM mission package is scheduled to achieve IOC in the fourth quarter of FY2015, and that Increment II of the ASW mission package is scheduled to achieve IOC in the fourth quarter of FY2016.[8] At an April 10, 2014, hearing on Navy shipbuilding programs before the Seapower subcommittee of the Senate Armed Services Committee, the Navy testified that

> The LCS Mission Modules program continues its efforts to field capability incrementally as individual mission systems become available, rather than wait for all the mission systems needed for the end-state capability. Beginning in March 2014, the program commenced Initial Operational Test and Evaluation (IOT&E) on the Surface Warfare (SUW) Mission Packages (MP). The Remote Minehunting System (RMS) completed its reliability growth program this past year and continues to test well. RMS supports the Mine Countermeasure (MCM) MP which expects to begin IOT&E in 2015. The ASW MP is planning a Preliminary Design Review in 2014 with IOT&E scheduled to begin in 2016. The LCS, with a MP, provides capability that is equal to or exceeds the current capability of the ships that it is replacing. The FY 2015 budget requests funding for three modules (1 MCM, 2 SUW).[9]

---

[6] Marinette Marine is a division of the Fincantieri Marine Group, an Italian shipbuilding firm. In 2009, Fincantieri purchased Manitowoc Marine Group, the owner of Marinette Marine and two other shipyards. Lockheed is a minority investor in Marinette Marine.

[7] Austal USA was created in 1999 as a joint venture between Austal Limited of Henderson, Western Australia, and Bender Shipbuilding & Repair Company of Mobile, AL, with Austal Limited as the majority owner.

[8] Department of Defense, *Department of Defense Fiscal Year (FY) 2015 Budget Estimates, Navy Justification Book Volume 2, Research, Development, Test & Evaluation, Navy, Budget Activity 4*, March 2014, pages 405-406 (pdf pages 467-468 of 770). See also pages 403-404 (pdf pages 465-466 of 770).

[9] Statement of The Honorable Sean J. Stackley, Assistant Secretary of the Navy (Research, Development and Acquisition), and Vice Admiral Joseph P. Mulloy, Deputy Chief of Naval Operations for Integration of Capabilities and Resources, and Vice Admiral William H. Hilarides, Commander, Naval Sea Systems Command, Before the Subcommittee on Seapower of the Senate Armed Services Committee on Department of the Navy Shipbuilding Programs, April 10, 2014, p. 11.

Manning and Deployment

Reduced-Size Crew

The LCS employs automation to achieve a reduced-sized core crew (i.e., sea frame crew). The program's aim was to achieve a core crew of 40 sailors, although the Navy has now decided to increase that number to about 50. Another 38 or so additional sailors are to operate the ship's embarked aircraft (about 23 sailors) and its embarked mission package (about 15 sailors in the case of the MCM package), which would make for a total crew of about 88 sailors (for an LCS equipped with an MCM mission package), compared to more than 200 for the Navy's frigates and about 300 (or more) for the Navy's current cruisers and destroyers.[10]

"3-2-1" Plan

The Navy plans to maintain three LCS crews for each two LCSs, and to keep one of those two LCSs continuously underway—a plan Navy officials refer to as "3-2-1." Under the 3-2-1 plan, LCSs are to be deployed for 16 months at a time, and crews are to rotate on and off deployed ships at 4-month intervals.[11] The 3-2-1 plan will permit the Navy to maintain a greater percentage of the LCS force in deployed status at any given time than would be possible under the traditional approach of maintaining one crew for each LCS and deploying LCSs for six to eight months at a time. The Navy plans to forward-station up to four LCSs in the Western Pacific at Singapore, and up to eight LCSs in the Persian Gulf at Bahrain.

Unit Procurement Cost Cap

LCS sea frames procured in FY2010 and subsequent years are subject to a unit procurement cost cap that can be adjusted to take inflation into account.[12] The Navy states that after taking inflation

---

[10] See *Report to Congress, Littoral Combat Ship Manning Concepts*, Prepared by OPNAV—Surface Warfare, July 2013 (with cover letters dated August 1, 2013), posted at USNI News on September 24, 2013, at http://news.usni.org/ 2013/09/24/document-littoral-combat-ship-manning-concepts.

[11] See, for example, Grace Jean, "Buying Two Littoral Combat Ship Designs Saves the Navy $600 Million, Official Says," *NationalDefenseMagazine.org*, January 12, 2011.

[12] The legislative history of the cost cap is as follows:

- The cost cap was originally established by Section 124 of the FY2006 National Defense Authorization act (H.R. 1815/P.L. 109-163 of January 6, 2006). Under this provision, the fifth and sixth ships in the class were to cost no more than $220 million each, plus adjustments for inflation and other factors.
- The cost cap was amended by Section 125 of the FY2008 National Defense Authorization Act (H.R. 4986/P.L. 110-181 of January 28, 2008). This provision amended the cost cap to $460 million per ship, with no adjustments for inflation, and applied the cap to all LCSs procured in FY2008 and subsequent years.
- The cost cap was amended again by Section 122 of the FY2009 Duncan Hunter National Defense Authorization Act (S. 3001/P.L. 110-417 of October 14, 2008). This provision deferred the implementation of the cost cap by two years, applying it to all LCSs procured in FY2010 and subsequent years.
- The cost cap was amended again by Section 121(c) and (d) of the FY2010 National Defense Authorization Act (H.R. 2647/P.L. 111-84 of October 28, 2009). The provision adjusted the cost cap to $480 million per ship, excluded certain costs from being counted against the $480 million cap, included provisions for adjusting the $480 million figure over time to take inflation and other events into account, and permitted the Secretary of the Navy to waive the cost cap under certain conditions. The Navy states that after taking inflation into account, the $480 million figure equates, as of December 2010, to $538 million.

Section 121(d)(1) states that the Secretary of the Navy may waive the cost cap if:

(continued...)

into account, the cost cap as of December 2010 was $538 million. In awarding the two LCS block buy contracts in December 2010 (see "2010 Dual-Award Acquisition Strategy (Implemented)" below), the Navy stated that LCSs to be acquired under the two contracts are to have an average unit cost of about $440 million, a figure well below the program's adjusted unit procurement cost cap (as of December 2010) of $538 million.[13]

Acquisition Cost

Sea Frames

The Navy's proposed FY2015 budget requests $1,427.1 million for three LCSs, or an average of about $475.7 million per ship.

The Department of Defense's (DOD's) December 31, 2012, Selected Acquisition Report (SAR) for the sea frame portion of the LCS program, which was released in late May 2013, estimates the total acquisition cost for 52 LCS sea frames at $33,955.5 million (i.e., about $34.0 billion) in then-year dollars. This figure includes $3,387.1 million in research and development costs (including funds for the construction of LCS-1 and LCS-2), $30,331.8 million in procurement costs for LCSs 3 through 52, and $236.6 million in military construction (MilCon) costs. In constant FY2010 dollars, these figures become $27,796.0 million, including $3,329.1 million in research and development costs, $24,266.9 million in procurement costs, and $200.0 million in MilCon costs, respectively.[14]

The estimated total acquisition cost of $33,955.5 million in then-year dollars reported in the December 31, 2012, SAR for the sea frame portion of the LCS program is $3,485.0 million less than the total of $37,440.5 million in then-year dollars reported in the December 31, 2011, SAR for the sea fame portion of the program. The estimated total acquisition cost of $27,796.0 million in constant FY2010 dollars reported in the December 31, 2012, SAR for the sea frame portion of the program is $2,881.5 million less than the $30,677.5 million in constant FY2010 dollars

---

(...continued)

    (A) the Secretary provides supporting data and certifies in writing to the congressional defense committees that—

        (i) the total amount obligated or expended for procurement of the vessel-

        (I) is in the best interest of the United States; and

        (II) is affordable, within the context of the annual naval vessel construction plan required by section 231 of title 10, United States Code; and

        (ii) the total amount obligated or expended for procurement of at least one other vessel authorized by subsection (a) has been or is expected to be less than $480,000,000; and

    (B) a period of not less than 30 days has expired following the date on which such certification and data are submitted to the congressional defense committees.

[13] Source: Contract-award information provided to CRS by navy office of Legislative Affairs, December 29, 2010. The 20 ships to be acquired under the two contracts have a target cost and a higher ceiling cost. Any cost growth above the target cost and up to the ceiling cost would be shared between the contractor and the Navy according to an agreed apportionment (i.e., a "share line"). Any cost growth above the ceiling cost would be borne entirely by the contractor. The Navy states that, as a worst case, if the costs of the 20 ships under the two FPI contracts grew to the ceiling figure and all change orders were expended, the average cost of the ships would increase by about $20 million, to about $460 million, a figure still well below the adjusted cost cap figure of $538 million.

[14] Department of Defense, *Selected Acquisition Report (SAR), LCS*, as of December 31, 2012, p. 14.

---

reported in the December 31, 2011, SAR for the sea frame portion of the program. The reduction of the program from a planned total of 55 ships to a planned total of 52 ships accounts for part of the reduction in the program's estimated total acquisition cost since the December 31, 2011, SAR.[15]

The December 31, 2012, SAR for the sea frame portion of the program reports an average unit procurement cost (APUC) for ships 3 through 52 of $485.3 million in constant FY2010 dollars, which is about 5.0% less than the APUC figure of $511.0 million in constant FY2010 dollars for ships 3 through 55 reported in the December 31, 2011, SAR for the sea frame portion of the program.[16]

Mission Packages

A March 2014 GAO report states that for a January 2014 Milestone B acquisition event, the LCS program office estimated the total acquisition cost of the LCS program's mission packages at $7.24 billion.[17] This figure does not account for any reductions in planned LCS mission package procurement that might result from the actions affecting the LCS program that were announced on February 24, 2014.

In August 2013, the Navy had stated that

> The estimated Average Production Unit Cost (APUC) for all 59 OPN-funded mission packages [the other five mission packages were funded through the Navy's research, development, test and evaluation (RDT&E) account] is $69.8M in Constant Year (CY) Fiscal Year 2010 dollars. This is the most accurate answer for "How much does it cost to buy a mission package?" These mission packages are production-representative assets for Operational Test and deployment. The LCS Mission Modules program will use OPN to procure 23 MCM mission packages, 21 SUW mission packages, 15 ASW mission packages, and 59 sets of common mission package equipment.
>
> The APUC can be broken down into the estimated average initial procurement cost of the three types of mission packages and common mission package equipment. None of the figures in this paper represent budget values.
>
> — Mine Countermeasures (MCM) Mission Packages (23): $97.7M

---

[15] Department of Defense, *Selected Acquisition Report (SAR), LCS*, as of December 31, 2012, pp. 31-32.

[16] Department of Defense, *Selected Acquisition Report (SAR), LCS*, as of December 31, 2012, p. 29.

[17] Government Accountability Office, *Defense Acquisitions[:] Assessments of Selected Weapon Programs*, GAO-14-340SP, March 2013, p. 96. See also Jason Sherman, "Navy Sets $7.2B Price Tag For Littoral Combat Ship Mission Modules," *Inside the Navy*, March 31, 2014.

The December 31, 2012, SAR for the sea frame portion of the LCS program does not contain estimated acquisition costs for the planned total of 64 LCS mission packages. The December 31, 2010, SAR for the LCS program stated:

> On February 18, 2011, USD(AT&L) [the Under Secretary of Defense (Acquisition, Technology, and Logistics)—DOD's acquisition executive] conducted a Milestone B (MS B) Defense Acquisition Board (DAB) for the seaframe portion of the LCS program. The decision of the DAB was to separate the program into two separate and distinct programs with separate reporting requirements. The Seaframe portion of the program is reported in this SAR as approved at MS B. The Mission Module portion of the program will begin reporting when it receives its Milestone B decision.
>
> (Department of Defense, *Selected Acquisition Report (SAR), LCS*, as of December 31, 2010, p. 4.)

— Surface Warfare (SUW) Mission Packages (21): $32.6M

— Anti-Submarine Warfare (ASW) Mission Packages (15): $20.9M

— Sets of Common Mission Package Equipment (59): $14.8M...

These estimates do not include the RDT&E expenditures that are associated with mission package development, integration, and test. These RDT&E expenditures include the five RDT&E-funded mission packages intended for use as development, training, and testing assets. Those five mission packages are not production-representative items. Including all prior RDT&E expenditures results in an average Program Acquisition Unit Cost of $99.7M for all 64 mission packages. This not an accurate answer for "How much does it cost to buy a mission package?" as past RDT&E expenditures are not relevant to the purchase price of a mission package today.[18]

Operation and Support (O&S) Cost

Sea Frames

DOD's December 31, 2012, SAR for the sea frame portion of the LCS program estimates the total life-cycle operation and support (O&S) cost for 55 sea frames (the previously planned total number),[19] each operated for 25 years, at $86,792.6 million (i.e., about $86.8 billion) in then-year dollars, or $50,334.6 million in constant FY2010 dollars. Included in this estimate are costs for 83 LCS sea frame crews (i.e., 3 crews for every two ships—see "Manning and Deployment" above) consisting of 40 core crew members each. The SAR estimates the annual O&S cost of a single LCS sea frame at $36.6 million in constant FY2010 dollars.[20] These figures do not account for the Navy's decision (see "Manning and Deployment" above) to increase the size of the LCS core crew to about 50.

A November 18, 2013, press report states:

> In the wake of a recent U.S. Government Accountability Office (GAO) report sparked by Aviation Week Intelligence Network (AWIN) stories, the U.S. Navy is striving for better cost estimates for its future Littoral Combat Ships (LCS).
>
> "In response to a recommendation in our July 2013 report, DOD now plans to do an independent cost estimate for the program before its next seaframe contract award in 2016," GAO says in a recent for-official-use-only report, "Littoral Combat Ships, Navy Needs to Address Communication System L imitations and Obtain Additional Operational and Cost Data," obtained by AWIN.

---

[18] Navy information paper on LCS program dated August 26, 2013, and provided to CRS and CBO on August 29, 2013.

[19] The December 31, 2012, states on page 42, "The Navy decision to reduce the procurement quantity of Seaframes from 55 to 52 was announced in January 2013 and did not provide enough time to develop and approve an associated Operating and Support (O&S) cost estimate. The updated O&S cost estimate reflecting the decrease in ship quantity will be reported in next year's SAR."

[20] Department of Defense, *Selected Acquisition Report (SAR), LCS*, as of December 31, 2012, p. 43.

Such an estimate is important, GAO says. "If the Navy follows the LCS Plan of Action and Milestones, it may contract for the entire fleet of ... LCS ships before actual operational information is obtained for both variants."...

The GAO notes: "The Navy plans to finalize its request for proposals for up to 28 additional LCS ships in late 2014, before it incorporates lessons learned from the USS Freedom deployment into the L CS CONOPS (concept of operations) or gains similar operational data for the Independence variant."

The Navy expects to consider contract proposals for additional LCS ships in early 2015 and to finalize the contract award in early 2016. "Although DOD said that it would update the seaframe cost estimate, there is no requirement to do so prior to 2016," GAO says.

But now the Pentagon has agreed to "identify actions and milestones to collect actual operational data on the second variant (Independence), and update operational support and sustainment cost estimates and strategy documents for both variants prior to contracting for additional LCS ships in 2016," GAO says.

The GAO explains that such updated data could put the program in a new light, given some of the programmatic changes thus far, such as the increase in the number of crewmembers and shore support staff. Part of the problems, GAO says, may be in the way the Navy calculated its initial cost estimates.

"In lieu of actual LCS data, the Navy used operations and support data from other surface ships, such as frigates, that were modified to approximate LCS characteristics to build the LCS cost estimate (referred to as modified analogous data)," GAO says. "For example, cost estimators used modified frigate data to estimate sustaining support costs such as munitions handling, and to estimate nonmaintenance supplies and equipment costs. Maintenance estimates were calculated by modifying analogous data from frigates and destroyers, among other ships, even though their maintenance concepts differ from those of the LCS."

Navy officials say that until they have actual operational data on both LCS seaframes, it is unknown whether the modified analogous cost data will reasonably correspond to actual LCS costs, according to GAO. The officials added that the seaframe estimate cannot be updated further without additional actual LCS operations and support data, including lessons learned from the USS Freedom's ongoing Singapore deployment. Navy liaison L t. Caroline Hutcheson says obtaining the needed data is one of the most important elements of Freedom's deployment.[21]

Mission Packages

The December 31, 2012, SAR for the sea frame portion of the LCS program does not contain estimated life-cycle O&S costs for the planned total of 64 LCS mission packages and the additional crew members that would be embarked on LCSs to operate them. As mentioned above in relation to mission package acquisition costs,[22] the December 31, 2010, SAR for the program stated:

---

[21] Michael Fabey, "U.S. Navy Seeking Independent LCS Cost Estimates," *Aerospace Daily & Defense Report*, November 18, 2013: 3.

[22] See the discussion in footnote 17.

On February 18, 2011, USD(AT&L)[23] conducted a Milestone B (MS B) Defense Acquisition Board (DAB) for the seaframe portion of the LCS program. The decision of the DAB was to separate the program into two separate and distinct programs with separate reporting requirements. The Seaframe portion of the program is reported in this SAR as approved at MS B. The Mission Module portion of the program will begin reporting when it receives its Milestone B decision.[24]

Major Program Developments Prior to February 24, 2014, DOD Announcement of Actions Affecting LCS Program

Growth in Sea Frame Procurement Costs

The Navy originally spoke of building LCS sea frames for about $220 million each in constant FY2005 dollars. Unit costs for the first few LCSs subsequently more than doubled. Costs for subsequent LCSs then came down under the current block buy contracts, to roughly $450 million each in current dollars, which equates to roughly $380 million in constant FY2005 dollars, using DOD's budget authority deflator for procurement excluding pay, fuel, and medical.[25] For a detailed discussion of cost growth on the first few LCS sea frames from the FY2007 budget through the FY2013 budget, see **Appendix A**.

2007 Program Restructuring and Ship Cancellations

The Navy substantially restructured the LCS program in 2007 in response to significant cost growth and delays in constructing the first LCS sea frames. This restructuring led to the cancellation in 2007 of four LCSs that were funded in FY2006 and FY2007. A fifth LCS, funded in FY2008, was cancelled in 2008. The annual procurement quantities shown above in **Table 1** reflect these cancellations (i.e., the five canceled ships no longer are shown in the annual procurement quantities in this table). For details on the 2007 program restructuring and the cancellation of the five LCSs funded in FY2006-FY2008, see **Appendix B**.

2009 Down Select Acquisition Strategy (Not Implemented)

On September 16, 2009, the Navy announced a proposed acquisition strategy under which the Navy would hold a competition to pick a single design to which all LCSs procured in FY2010 and subsequent years would be built (i.e., carry out a design "down select").[26] Section 121(a) and

---

[23] The Under Secretary of Defense (Acquisition, Technology, and Logistics)—DOD's acquisition executive.

[24] Department of Defense, *Selected Acquisition Report (SAR), LCS*, as of December 31, 2010, p. 4.

[25] This deflator is shown in *National Defense Budget Estimates for FY 2014*, May 2013, Table 5-7 (pages 71-72). This DOD budget reference document is also known as the "Green Book."

[26] The winner of the down select would be awarded a contract to build 10 LCSs over the five-year period FY2010-FY2014, at a rate of two ships per year. The Navy would then hold a second competition—open to all bidders other than the shipyard building the 10 LCSs in FY2010-FY2014—to select a second shipyard to build up to five additional LCSs to the same design in FY2012-FY2014 (one ship in FY2012, and two ships per year in FY2013-FY2014). These two shipyards would then compete for contracts to build LCSs procured in FY2015 and subsequent years.

Prior to the Navy's announcement of September 16, 2009, the Navy had announced an acquisition strategy for LCSs to be procured in FY2009 and FY2010. Under this acquisition strategy, the Navy bundled together the two LCSs funded in FY2009 (LCSs 3 and 4) with the three LCSs to be requested for FY2010 into a single, five-ship solicitation. The (continued...)

(b) of the FY2010 National Defense Authorization Act (H.R. 2647/P.L. 111-84 of October 28, 2009) provided the Navy authority to implement this down select strategy. The Navy's down select decision was expected to be announced by December 14, 2010, the date when the two LCS bidders' bid prices would expire.[27] The down select strategy was not implemented; it was superseded in late December 2010 by the current dual-award acquisition strategy (see next section). For additional background information on the down select strategy, see **Appendix C**.

2010 Dual-Award Acquisition Strategy (Implemented)

On November 3, 2010, while observers were awaiting the Navy's decision under the down select strategy (see previous section), the Navy notified congressional offices that it was prepared to implement an alternative dual-award acquisition strategy under which the Navy would forego making a down select decision and instead award each LCS bidder a 10-ship block buy contract for the six-year period FY2010-FY2015, in annual quantities of 1-1-2-2-2-2.[28] The Navy stated that, compared to the down select strategy, the dual-award strategy would reduce LCS procurement costs by hundreds of millions of dollars. The Navy needed additional legislative authority from Congress to implement the dual-award strategy. The Navy stated that if the additional authority were not granted by December 14, the Navy would proceed to announce its down select decision under the acquisition strategy announced on September 16, 2009. On December 13, 2010, it was reported that the two LCS bidders, at the Navy's request, had extended the prices in their bids to December 30, 2010, effectively giving Congress until then to decide whether to grant the Navy the authority needed for the dual-award strategy.

The Navy's November 3, 2010, proposal of a dual-award strategy posed an issue for Congress of whether this strategy would be preferable to the down select strategy, and whether Congress should grant the Navy, by December 30, 2010, the additional legislative authority the Navy would need to implement the dual-award strategy. On December 14, 2010, the Senate Armed Services Committee held a hearing to review the proposed dual-award strategy. Congress granted the Navy authority to implement the dual-award strategy in Section 150 of H.R. 3082/P.L. 111-322 of

---

(...continued)

Navy announced that each LCS industry team would be awarded a contract for one of the FY2009 ships, and that the prices that the two teams bid for both the FY2009 ships and the FY2010 ships would determine the allocation of the three FY2010 ships, with the winning team getting two of the FY2010 ships and the other team getting one FY2010 ship. This strategy was intended to use the carrot of the third FY2010 ship to generate bidding pressure on the two industry teams for both the FY2009 ships and the FY2010 ships.

The Navy stated that the contracts for the two FY2009 ships would be awarded by the end of January 2009. The first contract (for Lockheed Martin, to build LCS-3) was awarded March 23, 2009; the second contract (for General Dynamics, to build LCS-4) was awarded May 1, 2009. The delay in the awarding of the contracts past the end-of-January target date may have been due in part to the challenge the Navy faced in coming to agreement with the industry teams on prices for the two FY2009 ships that would permit the three FY2010 ships to be built within the $460 million LCS unit procurement cost cap. See also Statement of RADM Victor Guillory, U.S. Navy Director of Surface Warfare, and RADM William E. Landay, III, Program Executive Officer Ships, and Ms. E. Anne Sandel, Program Executive Officer Littoral and Mine Warfare, before the Subcommittee on Seapower and Expeditionary Forces of the House Armed Services Committee [hearing] on the Current Status of the Littoral Combat Ship Program, March 10, 2009, pp. 7-8.

[27] The Navy had earlier planned to make the down select decision and award the contract to build the 10 LCSs in the summer of 2010, but the decision was delayed to as late as December 14. (The final bids submitted by the two LCS contractors were submitted on about September 15, and were valid for another 90 days, or until December 14.)

[28] For more on block buy contracts, see CRS Report R41909, *Multiyear Procurement (MYP) and Block Buy Contracting in Defense Acquisition: Background and Issues for Congress*, by Ronald O'Rourke and Moshe Schwartz.

December 22, 2010, an act that, among other things, funded federal government operations through March 4, 2011.

On December 29, 2010, using the authority granted in H.R. 3082/P.L. 111-322, the Navy implemented the dual-award strategy, awarding a 10-ship, fixed-price incentive (FPI) block-buy contract to Lockheed, and another 10-ship, FPI block-buy contract to Austal USA. As mentioned earlier (see "Unit Procurement Cost Cap"), in awarding the contracts, the Navy stated that LCSs to be acquired under the two contracts are to have an average unit cost of about $440 million, a figure well below the program's adjusted unit procurement cost cap (as of December 2010) of $538 million. The 20 ships to be acquired under the two contracts have a target cost and a higher ceiling cost. Any cost growth above the target cost and up to the ceiling cost would be shared between the contractor and the Navy according to an agreed apportionment (i.e., a "share line"). Any cost growth above the ceiling cost would be borne entirely by the contractor. The Navy stated that, as a worst case, if the costs of the 20 ships under the two FPI contracts grew to the ceiling figure and all change orders were expended, the average cost of the ships would increase by about $20 million, to about $460 million, a figure still well below the adjusted cost cap figure of $538 million.[29]

The Navy on December 29, 2010, technically awarded only two LCSs (one to each contractor). These ships (LCS-5 and LCS-6) are the two LCSs funded in FY2010. Awards of additional ships under the two contracts are subject to congressional authorization and appropriations. The Navy states that if authorization or sufficient funding for any ship covered under the contracts is not provided, or if the Navy is not satisfied with the performance of a contractor, the Navy is not obliged to award additional ships covered under contracts. The Navy states that it can do this without paying a penalty to the contractor, because the two block-buy contracts, unlike a typical multiyear procurement (MYP) contract, do not include a provision requiring the government to pay the contractor a contract cancellation penalty.[30]

For additional background information on the dual-award strategy, see **Appendix D**.

Changes in Mission Package Equipment

The Navy since January 2011 has announced changes to the composition of all three LCS mission packages. The concept for the ASW package, and consequently the equipment making up the package, was changed substantially. The equipment making up the MIW package has changed somewhat, partly as a result of the testing of the MIW systems being developed for the package. An Army-developed missile called Non-Line of Sight Launch System (NLOS-LS) that was to be used in the SUW package was canceled by the Army and has been replaced for the next few years in the LCS SUW module by the shorter-ranged Army Longbow Hellfire missile, pending the eventual acquisition for the LCS SUW module of a follow-on missile with longer range.[31]

---

[29] Source: Contract-award information provided to CRS by navy office of Legislative Affairs, December 29, 2010.

[30] Source: Navy briefing to CRS and the Congressional Budget Office (CBO) on December 15, 2010. For a press article on this issue, see Cid Standifer, "FY-11 LCS Contracts On Hold Because Of Continuing Resolution," *Inside the Navy*, March 14, 2011.

[31] The Navy initially chose the Griffin missile as the near-term replacement for NLOS-LS, but in April 2014 announced that the near-term replacement for NLOS-LS would instead be the Longbow Hellfire missile. See Sam LaGrone, "Navy Axes Griffin Missile In Favor of Longbow Hellfire for LCS," *USNI News* (http://news.usni.org), April 9, 2014; Mike McCarthy, "LCS Program Dumping Griffin Missile In Favor Of Army's Longbow," *Defense Daily*, April 10, 2014; (continued...)

2012 Establishment of LCS Council

On August 22, 2012, Admiral Jonathan Greenert, the chief of Naval Operations, established an LCS Council headed by four vice admirals to address challenges faced by the LCS program for supporting the planned deployment of an LCS to Singapore beginning in 2013. The challenges were identified in four internal Navy reviews of the LCS program (two of them based on wargames) that were completed between February and August of 2012. The memorandum from the CNO establishing the council states that the council will be "empowered ... to drive action across the acquisition, requirements and Fleet enterprises of the Navy." The council was given an immediate focus of developing and implementing an LCS plan of action and milestones by January 31, 2013. The memorandum also required the council to develop a charter for its operations within 14 days.[32] The charter for the council, dated September 2012, states that

> The LCS program's unique requirements, rapid acquisition, and innovative manning and sustainment strategies pose unique challenges as LCS is introduced to the fleet. The Council will rapidly and decisively resolve impediments to the LCS program's success, determine the way forward for the future evolution of LCS capabilities, and inform senior Navy civilian and uniformed leadership of key issues which require decisions at the highest level....

> The LCS Council will drive actions across the requirements, acquisition, and Fleet enterprises of the Navy to ensure the successful procurement, development, manning, training, sustainment, and operational employment of the LCS Class ships, their associated Mission Packages, and shore infrastructure.

> The LCS Council provides oversight and direction of the efforts required at all echelons of the administrative chain of command to achieve successful fleet introduction of LCS, to identify and resolve challenges and impediments, and to evolve the program. The Council is constituted and empowered to bridge "gaps and seams" that may exist or arise between various LCS stakeholders, warfare and mission communities, and supporting activities.[33]

Controversy and Proposals to Truncate the Program

The LCS program has been controversial due to past cost growth, design and construction issues with the lead ships built to each design, concerns over the ships' ability to withstand battle damage, and concerns over whether the ships are sufficiently armed and would be able to perform their stated missions effectively. Prior to Secretary Hagel's February 24, 2014, announcement, some observers, citing one or more of these issues, had proposed truncating the LCS program to either 24 ships (i.e., stopping procurement after procuring all the ships covered under the two

---

(...continued)

Michael Fabey, "Hellfire Front-Runner For U.S. Navy Littoral Combat Ship," *Aerospace Daily & Defense Report*, April 10, 2014: 4.

[32] Memorandum from Chief of Naval Operations to Director, Navy Staff, dated August 22, 2012, on Lilttoral Combat Ship (LCS) Council, posted at *InsideDefense.com* (subscription required), August 24, 2012. See also Defense Media Activity—Navy, "CNO Establishes LCS Council," *Navy News Service*, August 22, 2012; Christopher P. Cavas, "U.S. Navy Creates LCS 'Council' To Guide Development," *DefenseNews.com*, August 22, 2012; Megan Eckstein, "CNO Establishes LCS Council To Review Recent Data, Lessons Learned," *Inside the Navy*, August 27, 2012; Mike McCarthy, "Navy Establishes LCS Council," *Defense Daily*, August 27, 2012.

[33] *Littoral Combat Ship Council Charter*, September 2012, posted at InsideDefense.com (subscription required), September 28, 2012, p. 3.

block buy contracts) or to some other number well short of 52.[34] Other observers have proposed down selecting to a single LCS design (i.e., continuing production of only one of the two designs) after the 24th ship.

In response to criticisms of the LCS program, the Navy has acknowledged certain problems and stated that it was taking action to correct them, disputed other arguments made against the program, and (until Hagel's February 24, 2014, announcement) maintained its support for completing the planned program of 52 ships. The August 2012 establishment of the LCS Council (see "2012 Establishment of LCS Council" above) might be viewed as a Navy response to certain criticisms of the program made by some observers.

The LCS is by no means the only Navy shipbuilding program to have encountered controversy over the years; several others have experienced controversy for one reason or another, with recent examples including the Gerald R. Ford (CVN-78) class aircraft carrier program (due to cost growth),[35] the Zumwalt (DDG-1000) class destroyer program (due to affordability and technical risk),[36] and the San Antonio (LPD-17) class amphibious ship program (due to cost growth and construction quality issues).[37]

February 24, 2014, DOD Announcement of Actions Affecting LCS Program

February 24, 2014, Address and Background Briefing

On February 24, 2014, in an address previewing certain decisions incorporated into DOD's FY2015 budget submission, Secretary of Defense Chuck Hagel stated:

> Regarding the Navy's littoral combat ship [LCS], I am concerned that the Navy is relying too heavily on the LCS to achieve its long-term goals for ship numbers. Therefore, no new contract negotiations beyond 32 ships will go forward. With this decision, the LCS line will continue beyond our five-year budget plan with no interruptions.
>
> The LCS was designed to perform certain missions—such as mine sweeping and anti-submarine warfare—in a relatively permissive environment. But we need to closely examine

---

[34] For example, a May 2012 report by the Center for a New American Security (CNAS) recommended stopping the LCS program in FY2017 after procuring a total of 27 ships (David W. Barno, et al, *Sustainable Pre-eminence[:] Reforming the U.S. Military at a Time of Strategic Change*, Center for a New American Security, May 2012, pp. 35, 67), and an April 2011 report by the Heritage Foundation recommended a future Navy fleet with a total of 28 small surface combatants—a category that appears to include both Oliver Hazard Perry (FFG-7) frigates (which are being phased out of service) and LCSs (*A Strong National Defense[:] The Armed Forces America Needs and What They Will Cost*, Heritage Foundation, April 5, 2011, pp. 25-26). CNAS made a similar recommendation in a report it published in October 2011 (David W. Barno, et al, *Hard Choices[:] Responsible Defense in an Age of Austerity*, Center for a New American Security, October 2011, pp. 13, 14, 15, 16, 18, 20, 21, 34, 35. The report recommends procuring a total of 27 LCSs under three DOD budget scenarios, or a total of 12 LCSs under a fourth DOD budget scenario).

[35] For more on the CVN-78 program, see CRS Report RS20643, *Navy Ford (CVN-78) Class Aircraft Carrier Program: Background and Issues for Congress*, by Ronald O'Rourke.

[36] For more on the DDG-1000 program, see CRS Report RL32109, *Navy DDG-51 and DDG-1000 Destroyer Programs: Background and Issues for Congress*, by Ronald O'Rourke.

[37] For more on the LPD-17 program, see CRS Report RL34476, *Navy LPD-17 Amphibious Ship Procurement: Background, Issues, and Options for Congress*, by Ronald O'Rourke.

whether the LCS has the independent protection and firepower to operate and survive against a more advanced military adversary and emerging new technologies, especially in the Asia Pacific. If we were to build out the LCS program to 52 ships, as previously planned, it would represent one- sixth of our future 300-ship Navy. Given continued fiscal restraints, we must direct shipbuilding resources toward platforms that can operate in every region and along the full spectrum of conflict.

Additionally, at my direction, the Navy will submit alternative proposals to procure a capable and lethal small surface combatant, generally consistent with the capabilities of a frigate. I've directed the Navy to consider a completely new design, existing ship designs, and a modified LCS. These proposals are due to me later this year in time to inform next year's budget submission.[38]

Also on February 24, 2014, in a background briefing associated with Hagel's address, a senior defense official stated:

On the LCS, we clearly do need the LCS capabilities of the minesweeps, the ASW [Anti-Submarine Warfare] module for example is looking very promising, and we absolutely need those capabilities. But as we look at our adversary growing capabilities, we also need to make certain that our fleet has enough capabilities, enough survivability and lethality that they can go up against those adversaries, so we want to look at what—what is out there for the future of the small surface combatants beyond LCS? And we—and we want to start that now.[39]

February 24, 2014, Memorandum to Navy Leadership

A February 24, 2014, memorandum from Secretary of Defense Hagel to Secretary of the Navy Ray Mabus and Chief of Naval Operations Admiral Jonathan Greenert stated:

I have given careful consideration to the Littoral Combat Ship (LCS) program, and I wanted to get back to you on my decision. I have consulted with Naval Surface Commanders, acquisition officials, policy and evaluation experts and reviewed preliminary assessments and evaluations of the LCS.

If we build out the LCS program to 52 ships it would represent one-sixth of our future 300-ship Navy. Given the emerging threat environment of the future, I have considerable reservations as to whether that is what our Navy will require over the next few decades. I recognize the importance of presence, which is tied to the number of ships. But I also believe that capability and power projection is the foundation of our Navy's effectiveness.

Therefore, no new contract negotiations beyond 32 ships will go forward. The Department of the Navy is directed to provide me the following information:

---

[38] DOD News Transcript, "Remarks by Secretary Hagel and Gen. Dempsey on the fiscal year 2015 budget preview in the Pentagon Briefing Room," February 24, 2014, accessed February 25, 2014, at http://www.defense.gov/transcripts/transcript.aspx?transcriptid=5377. Brackets as in original.

[39] DOD News Transcript, "Background Briefing on Fiscal 2015 Budget Recommendations," February 24, 2014, accessed February 25, 2014, at http://www.defense.gov/transcripts/transcript.aspx?transcriptid=5376. Brackets as in original.

— Provide regular updates on LCS performance based on test results and experience from recent deployments. These assessments should consider survivability, performance, sustainment cost, materiel readiness, lethality and growth potential.

— Submit to me, in time to inform the PB 2016 [President's Budget for FY2016] budget deliberations, alternative proposals to procure a capable and lethal small surface combatant, generally consistent with the capabilities of a frigate. Options considered should include a completely new design, existing ship designs (including the LCS), and a modified LCS. Include target cost, mission requirements, sensors and weapon requirements and required delivery date.

If a modified LCS is an acceptable option for a more capable small surface combatant, negotiations for LCS beyond the 24 ships currently on contract should seek to incorporate the upgraded LCS as soon as possible. Should the aforementioned assessments provide dispositive against the LCS, I retain the right to modify the program.

As we both agree, smart investments in our future ships will be required as we continue to face limited resources over the next few years. We need to focus on what the Navy will require in the years ahead to meet our Nation's security needs and future missions.[40]

Earlier Press Reports That DOD Was Considering Truncating Program

DOD's February 24, 2014, announcement of actions affecting the LCS program followed press reports dating back to September 2013 that DOD was considering truncating the program.[41] In response to these press reports, the Navy reiterated its support for a 52-ship LCS program.[42] Sean Stackley, the Navy's acquisition executive (i.e., the Assistant Secretary of the Navy for Research, Development, and Acquisition), was quoted as stating on January 16, 2014, that "We have a valid requirement for 52 ships, and the program is performing strongly," and that "the Navy's position on the LCS program is that it is solid."[43]

Navy Work to Identify Ship to Follow 32 LCSs

Navy Testimony and Letter

At an April 10, 2014, hearing on Navy shipbuilding programs before the Seapower subcommittee of the Senate Armed Services Committee, the Navy testified that

---

[40] Memorandum dated February 24, 2014, from the Office of the Secretary of Defense to the Secretary of the Navy and Chief of Naval Operations on Littoral Combat Ship (LCS) program, posted at InsideDefense.com (subscription required) February 28, 2014.

[41] See Christopher P. Cavas, "Sources: Pentagon Backs Cutting LCS to 24 Ships," *DefenseNews.com*, September 2, 2013; Christopher P. Cavas, "Pentagon Cuts LCS Buy to 32 Ships," *DefenseNews.com*, January 15, 2014; Tony Capaccio, "Pentagon Said to Order Cutting Littoral Ships by 20," *Bloomberg News*, Jan. 15, 2014.

[42] Nathan Phelps, "US Navy Secretary Says He's Committed to LCS," *DefenseNews.com*, September 13, 2013.

[43] Carlo Munoz, "SNA 2014: 52-Ship LCS Requirement is 'Solid,'" *USNI News* (http://news.usni.org), January 16, 2014. See also Kris Osborn, "Navy Still Expects to Build 52 Ship LCS Fleet," *DoD Buzz* (*www.dodbuzz.com*), January 16, 2014; Mike McCarthy, "Navy Acquisition Chief Insists Need For 52 LCSs Is Firm," *Defense Daily*, January 17, 2014: 2; and Olga Belogolova, "Navy Officials Stand By 52-Ship Requirement For Embattled LCS Program," *Inside the Navy*, January 20, 2014.

While the Navy continues to focus on the merits of LCS and the capabilities it brings to the fleet, the service also recognizes the importance of maintaining awareness of emerging threats and capabilities of our Nation's adversaries. As a result, the Navy is examining options to increase the lethality of our small surface combatant force. Specifically, the Navy is studying existing ship designs (including the LCS), a modified LCS, and a completely new ship design, including their estimated cost, to determine the most affordable method for improving the capability of this critical element of our force. Pending the results of this study (due in support of FY 2016 budget formulation), the Navy will restrict LCS contract actions within the first 32 ships of the class.[44]

A March 13, 2014, joint letter from Admiral Greenert and Sean Stackley, the Assistant Secretary of the Navy for Research, Development, and Acquisition (i.e., the Navy's acquisition executive), to other Navy recipients outlined the work to be done to identify the ship that is to follow the first 32 LCSs:

This letter... identifies a core Navy team (Small Surface Combatant Task Force (SSCTF)) to execute the task. The SSCTF findings will be delivered to the Chief of Naval Operations (CNO) and the Assistant Secretary of the Navy (Research, Development and Acquisition) (ASN(RDA)) no later than (NLT) July 31, 2014. Interim reporting requirements will be directed by CNO and ASN(RDA)....

The SSCTF will... develop an analysis plan for approval by CNO and ASN(RDA) NLT March 31, 2014, which should include the actions below in developing alternative proposals for a small surface combatant:

a. Establish the requirements and requirements trade space of a small surface combatant in accordance with [Secretary of Defense Hagel's February 24, 2014, memo to the Secretary of the Navy and the CNO]. For purposes of establishing an initial baseline, the SSCTF shall generate a side-by-side comparison of the FFG 7 [Oliver Hazard Perry] Class requirements/capabilities versus the Littoral Combat Ship (LCS) Class requirements/capabilities. In addition, the SSCTF shall characterize the emerging threat environment, consistent with the current Force Structure Assessment, and identify gaps that may necessitate requirements changes for a future small surface combatant.

b. Assess the impact of the requirements delta to LCS (both sea frames).

c. Translate the requirements delta into design concepts for a small surface combatant, considering the folowing alternatives:

(1) Modified LCS design.

(2) Existing ship design.

(3) New ship design.

d. Include with each design concept:

---

[44] Statement of The Honorable Sean J. Stackley, Assistant Secretary of the Navy (Research, Development and Acquisition) and Vice Admiral Joseph P. Mulloy, Deputy Chief of Naval Operations for Integration of Capabilities and Resources and Vice Admiral William H. Hilarides, Commander, Naval Sea Systems Command, Before the Subcommittee on Seapower of the Senate Armed Services Committee on Department of the Navy Shipbuilding Programs, April 10, 2014, pp. 11-12.

(1) Top level requirements (including sensors, weapons, combat system requirements).

(2) Cost.

(3) Major milestone schedule.

(4) The lethality of the ship to air, surface and undersea threats....

In our efforts to increase the capability and lethality of the Small Surface Combatant force, affordability must remain a critical tenet that informs and guides our decision. Accordingly, an affordability target will be established under separate tasking and provided to the SSCTF.[45]

At a March 26, 2014, hearing on the Navy's proposed FY2015 budget before the Seapower and Projection Forces subcommittee of the House Armed Services Committee, the following exchange occurred:

> REPRESENTATIVE J. RANDY FORBES, CHAIRMAN (continuing): ... The last question I have is has DOD performed a new analysis of mission needs to identify what capability gaps the Navy might need to address the new shipbuilding program to replace the littoral combat ship?
>
> If not, then how can DOD know that it needs a new ship generally consistent with the capabilities of a frigate? Where's the properly validated requirements for this new program?
>
> SEAN STACKLEY, ASSISTANT SECRETARY OF THE NAVY FOR RESEARCH, DEVELOPMENT, AND ACQUISITION: I'm going to start and then Admiral Mulloy will finish. The requirements for the LCS program are well documented. And right now we're moving smartly through the execution of that program in terms of the basic hull and then the mission packages.
>
> What the secretary of defense described in his guidance to us, and then his subsequent announcement was that the department is looking to increase the lethality of the LCS and something similar to a frigate.
>
> So we are—we do have a requirements team taking a hard look at exactly what would that mean. What missions, what roles, what is the concept of operations looking forward beyond the first 32 to those next 20 small surface combatants? What is that concept of operations in the additional lethality that it would require similar to a frigate?
>
> I don't want to predetermine the outcome of that review. The team frankly is locked up in a worm [sic: war room][46] that we have set aside.
>
> What I would welcome and invite is your staff to visit, to join, to take a look at the process, to take a look their findings and findings along the way. And this then will be used as we put together our [fiscal year] 2016 budget and look at either modifying the LCS or if need be a new ship class.

---

[45] Joint letter dated March 13, 2014, from the Chief of Naval Operations and the Assistant Secretary of the Navy (Research, Development, and Acquisition) on Small Surface Combatant Task Force, posted at InisideDefense.com (subscription required) March 18, 2014.

[46] "War room" is a term used by people in the defense community to mean a room in which the occupants focus on exploring a particular issue or set of issues over a certain period of time.

In either case when it comes to modifying an LCS we've always contemplated future flights of LCS. So this could be a very simple, straightforward, in-stride modification just like we do with other ship classes. If it equates to a new ship class, that's a very different picture.

And so again, just like every other discussion we've had today, a piece of this requirements definition is going to include affordability. So we have to strike the right balance between what is that degree of added lethality, added capability to an LCS that we need for CONOPS which we will be operating, which includes with the rest of the battle force.

And then what does that mean in terms of cost? And what does that mean in terms of schedule? When will we be able to introduce that capability for the small service combatant?

FORBES: Caught between two very powerful currents that both want to go in different directions. I don't know where the subcommittee ends up coming out, but we've got to make sure they have the right analysis so they can make that decision.

Admiral?

VICE ADMIRAL JOSEPH MULLOY, DEPUTY CHIEF OF NAVAL OPERATIONS FOR INTEGRATION OF CAPABILITIES AND RESOURCES: Yes, sir. What I would say is the requirements paperwork almost has to come after. But as the secretary pointed out, we do a lot of changes in other classes of ships.

I mean as you look at the [attack submarine North Dakota, the first in Flight IV [of the Virginia-class submarine program]. I mean the flight we're doing now in South Dakota is there's been changes. I mean North Dakota's being built with vertical launch tubes and the bow and a wraparound ray (ph) [sic: array, meaning sonar array].

Nothing to do with the original Menzen Org (ph) [sic: mission ORD, meaning Operational Requirements Document] when the Virginia was designed had that in it. Yet the combat power and the design of that ship is fundamentally changing.

Flight III Burkes [i.e., DDG-51 destroyers] are not having a whole new set [of requirements documentation]. But they're fundamentally different than Flight I when the Burke was built.

So the Navy has a pattern of making changes to improve ships. So we really have to get the tiger team—which I have some of my people on the staff, Admiral Coin (ph) does, Major Stackley (inaudible) was the leader—is this key component.

And then is it a change to the ship? Is it a whole new ship? Either way we can write some paperwork faster than we have to.

I have a copy of the Nautilus [i.e., the first nuclear-powered submarine] initial paperwork design written by in the 1950s, six pages long to build naval nuclear power. It is not the document you would see that had Virginia-class.

So I'm not sure we have to go back to six pages. But I know we can work faster on that once we define what we have. And I think some of your staff coming to see this team or meet some of the people would be outstanding because the secretary's taking it very seriously that we need to figure out what those next 20 are.

But we need small service combatants going back to the FSA [force structure assessment] design is small service combatants fill a range of needs. They're not all at the high end, but they magnify and amplify phase one convoys, ASW.

They also support phase zero [day-to-day, pre-crisis] operations around the world and engagement. And that's what we need to go back to. What does the ship have to bring and what does it have to have for the higher end capability, but mesh it into the whole class.[47]

In remarks he made to reporters after the hearing, Stackley stated, "The guidance from SECDEF was fairly broad—frigate-like, increased lethality, consider LCS, modified LCS, some other existing ship design or a new ship design.... And so we want to make sure that we stay to that top level guidance in terms of what additional capability and the framework of how is the ship going to be employed and the framework of what's affordable."[48]

Press Reports

A February 24, 2014, press report that was posted after Hagel's February 24 address states that the Navy "has already begun in earnest" to work on the ship that is to follow the 32 LCSs. The report stated: "The Navy will begin a capabilities-based assessment in the next few months on the new platform to set the ship up for the start of the acquisition process." The report stated that following a conference held in January 2013 (i.e., 13 months before DOD's February 24, 2014, announcement), the Navy "began a 90-day wargame to define modularity, scalability and flexibility for the future surface combatant." The report quoted a Navy official as stating on February 20, 2014, that the Navy commissioned a study on the future surface combatant that was performed from August 2013 to December 2013.[49]

A March 7, 2014, press report states:

> The Navy is in the early phases of a new study designed to explore alternative proposals for the Littoral Combat Ship formally requested last week by Defense Secretary Chuck Hagel, Navy officials said.
>
> The study will explore the realm of the possible regarding potential new platforms for LCS and modifications to existing LCS ships, per guidance from Hagel. It will be headed by Naval Sea Systems Command, or NAVSEA, and the Navy's requirements community for surface warfare.
>
> The current study is beginning to look at a range of options, including adding more armament and weaponry to the LCS, or designing a new platform able to accommodate more armor, weapons and vertical launch tubes for missiles, service officials said....
>
> The study is also looking at existing foreign variants of the LCS, some of which are larger and configured differently than U.S. versions.
>
> "All of the things that are out there will be part of the market place of ideas," a Navy official said.

---

[47] Transcript of hearing.

[48] As quoted in Olga Belogolova, "Small Surface Combatant Task Force Not Setting Affordability Target," *Inside the Navy*, March 31, 2014.

[49] Olga Belogolova and Lee Hudson, "Pentagon Tasks Navy To Look Beyond LCS At A 'Future Surface Combatant,'" *InsideDefense.com (Defense Alert)*, February 24, 2014.

The mission of LCS is a fundamental focus of the study, because the alternative proposals could lead to specs for a new, heavier and larger ship that is more heavily armed and closer to a frigate.

Or, the Navy could build upon the mine and submarine hunting technologies built onto the current LCS platform. In fact, the alternative proposal effort may seek to combine these attributes into a single ship.

"Not every ship can do everything, so what are the missions we want to focus on?" a Navy official said....

The LCS mission module concept may be preserved for the alternative proposals, service officials said. As currently configured, the LCS has three different integrated sets or suites of technologies for surface warfare, mine-hunting and anti-submarine missions.

Vice Adm. Joseph Mulloy, Deputy Chief of Naval Operation for Integration of Capabilities and Resources, recently said the Navy will work on alternative proposals for the ship in light of guidance from Defense Secretary Chuck Hagel.

"I view this as a chance for the Navy to re-engage on what's important to us on the last part of the class. We know we need mine hunting, we know we need ASW (anti-submarine warfare), we know we need a few of what's called the surface warfare module – but what do we really need? We are going to go back and take a hard look and respond to the Secretary of Defense in the fall," said Mulloy.[50]

A March 10, 2014, press report states:

Under orders to reexamine the Littoral Combat Ship program and begin the process of evaluating possible new designs, Adm. Jon Greenert, chief of naval operations, said Monday [March 10] he was preparing to stand up a new task force to provide him with recommendations....

The new task force will supersede the LCS Council, a group of high-ranking officers assembled in August 2012 to help guide the program. Under the guidance of the director of the Navy Staff, Vice Adm. Richard Hunt, the council issued directives and gave the program a new high-profile emphasis.

But its actions largely fell out of sight after Hunt's retirement last summer, and his successor, Vice Adm. Michelle Howard, never spoke publicly in a council role. She has since moved on to a deputy CNO position, and has been nominated to become the vice chief of naval operations....

Greenert, speaking to reporters at the Pentagon on Monday, said he would issue a memo "shortly" that would describe the makeup of the new task force. He did not reveal what office would be leading the effort.

"There will be people in the [Naval Sea Systems Command] end of this, people in the requirements end," he said.

"We're going to kind of look at it like the Marine Corps did their amphibious combat vehicle recently," the CNO added. "They got some real good integration and systems engineers to

---

[50] Kris Osborn, "Navy Starts Study to Re-Examine LCS Mission," *DoD Buzz* (*www.dodbuzz.com*), March 7, 2014.

take a look at it. You can start with naval architects, but how does it come together? Those are the people who have to be key to this, in addition to capabilities."

Greenert noted that "the LCS Council was always meant to be temporary. I'm getting ready to step it down. It's not gone yet, but stay tuned."[51]

An April 14, 2014, press report states:

The Navy does not have the time to develop a wholly new design for a small surface combatant, one of the options being looked at by a Navy task force set up to address survivability and lethality gaps associated with the Littoral Combat Ship program, a top Navy official said last week.

At the Navy League's annual Sea-Air-Space symposium... on April 7, Vice Adm. Tom Copeman, naval surface forces commander for the U.S. Pacific Fleet, said that he does not expect the service to settle on a new design for the future small surface combatant.[52]

An April 19, 2014, press report states:

Ships that look like littoral combat ships (LCS), but armed with SM-2 surface-to-air missiles, bigger guns and Aegis combat systems. A grey-hull patrol frigate that takes the hull of a white coast guard cutter and increases its combat power.

With an eye to the international market, shipbuilders Lockheed Martin, Austal USA and Huntington Ingalls have worked to develop more heavily armed versions of ships already in production for domestic customers. Now, ironically, the proposals might have their best chance yet—as the choice to succeed the LCS as the US Navy's next small surface combatant (SSC)....

Industry teams are hard at work trying to anticipate what the [Navy's Small Surface Combatant] task force will look for. So who's got the inside track?

There seems to be little likelihood a new design will be chosen. There is little money to begin a development effort, and a new design generally takes more than a decade to put into production and field. Critics already are frustrated that the LCS program has only one significant deployment thus far, after more than 12 years in development.

Fans of the [Oliver Hazard Perry] FFG 7 [frigate design] are also likely to be frustrated. Even if a similar ship were chosen, hundreds of standards have changed significantly, virtually turning such an effort into a new-design prospect. No go.

Several foreign shipbuilders, such as Italy's Fincantieri and Spain's Navantia, might also be interested, but even though both existing LCS designs are derived from foreign sources, the likelihood a mature non-US design would be chosen is very low.

Political pressures for some sort of increased armament also seem to argue against the chance no major LCS design changes will be made.

---

[51] Christopher P. Cavas, "CNO: Group Will Study New LCS Designs," *DefenseNews.com*, March 10, 2014. The bracketed term "[Naval Sea Systems Command]" as in original.

[52] Olga Belogolova, "Top Navy Official: New Design For A Small Surface Combatant Unlikely," *Inside the Navy*, April 14, 2014.

The field of contenders, then, would seem to be limited to those with ships currently in production: Lockheed Martin, Austal USA and—perhaps—Huntington Ingalls Industries (HII).[53]

A May 2, 2014, press report states that "the U.S. Navy has made it clear that it intends to start with essentially a clean sheet in developing the Small Surface Combatant (SSC) that will succeed the Littoral Combat Ship (LCS).... " The report also states that "the shortened time for [submitting and evaluating proposals] leads many analysts to believe the Navy will likely come out with a ship very similar to LCS, or a modified version of the two existing LCS classess.... "[54]

A May 21, 2014, press report states that Admiral Jonathan Greenert, the Chief of Naval Operations, in remarks to reporters that day,

> cast Hagel's order—to determine whether the Navy should build an improved current-model LCS or an all-new frigate-type design—as part of a long-standing practice in shipbuilding.
>
> "All of our classes—our Perry-class [frigates] had four flights, our Spruance-class [destroyers] had at least two flights, our Arleigh Burke-class [destroyers] will have what will amounts to four flights—there's obviously a pattern here," he said. "We never really articulated formally or discussed the feasibility of having flights of our Littoral Combat Ship, and how we intended to upgrade the ships."...
>
> "It would appear to me we could—and should—have been more clear to him, so he wrote us a memo to make sure that we could be very clear, within the department, on how we would go ahead," the admiral said....
>
> [Greenert] defended the basic wisdom of the LCS: To field a relatively small, fast ship that can take aboard different sets of mission equipment, as opposed to carrying the built-in weapons and sensors of a traditional warship.
>
> The LCS is still ahead of the game as compared with a legacy ship, he said, given that it can take 20 years to go from designing to fielding a traditional design.
>
> Skeptics in Congress and elsewhere in the Pentagon, though, don't share that same kind of enthusiasm....
>
> But the Navy has gained a highly placed ally with the Senate confirmation of Deputy Defense Secretary Robert Work, an outspoken LCS advocate who took the place of an outspoken LCS skeptic in his predecessor, acting Deputy Secretary Christine Fox.
>
> Fox is understood to have been a driving force behind the senior-level push for the Navy to buy a more robust frigate-type warship, as opposed to the existing LCS. Work, on the other hand, became one of the original voices behind the interpretation that Greenert adopted on Wednesday [May 21]: Hagel's order wasn't a rebuke of a disappointing program, but rather an encouragement for the Navy to take the prudent next step, often called "spiral development."

---

[53] Christopher P. Cavas, "Ship Study Should Favor Existing Designs," *DefenseNews.com*, April 19, 2014.

[54] Michael Fabey, "LCS Template Colors Small Surface Combatant Development," *Aerospace Daily & Defense Report*, May 2, 2014: 1-2.

That had been a part of the Navy's internal understanding all along, Greenert said, and now Hagel's order enables everyone in the Pentagon to get onto the same page.

"I think within the Navy we were comfortable," Greenert said. "But outside the Navy, clearly, within the department, people had different opinions. ... So to me, this is a great opportunity to sit down, when we're done with this, stack hands and say: 'This is where we're going, the decision has been made by the secretary of Defense, and it'll be embedded in our '16 budget.'"[55]

A May 23, 2014, press report states:

Modified Littoral Combat Ships (LCS) with more firepower and a design based on the U.S. Coast Guard's National Security Cutter were among the concepts passed along to the Navy on Thursday [May 22] as the service seeks information intended to guide its requirements for a small surface combatant....

"I can confirm that General Dynamics Bath Iron Works submitted a response to the RFI," said Jim DeMartini, a spokesman for Bath Iron Works, which currently builds two classes of Navy destroyers. "We are not providing further details."

Lockheed Martin said its response leverages the investment already made in the Freedoms, and that its design is adaptable for upgrades and can be scaled to a larger ship. Joe North, vice president of Lockheed Martin littoral ship systems, said the options outlined also include surface-to-surface missiles, launchers and improved radar while keeping the ship unit cost below $700 million....

Terry O'Brien, vice president of business development and external affairs at Austal USA, said the company submitted a response to the Navy's RFIs that is an improved version of Independence for anti-submarine warfare, including a towed sonar array and torpedoes. It would also add the vertically launched anti-submarine rocket (ASROC), and a "tremendous" aviation capability to support the MH-60 helicopter. The improvement to the surface capability includes a 76 mm gun as well as remotely operated smaller ones, a vertically launched surface-to-air missile as well as improved radar fire-and-engage capability.

Bill Glenn, a spokeswoman for Huntington Ingalls Industries, said its Ingalls Shipbuilding yard proposed a hull based on the National Security Cutter the firm is building for the U.S. Coast Guard. He called it a "high performance, proven hull and propulsion system that is a lethal, survivable and affordable design for the small surface combatant."[56]

A June 2, 2014, press report states:

Companies interested in pursuing the Navy's follow on for the small surface combatant requirement will have to come close to the current cost of building Littoral Combat Ship (LCS), the chief of Naval Sea Systems Command (NAVSEA) said this week....

Vice Adm. William Hilarides would not discuss details of the industry responses, but told a group of reporters Thursday that cost will be a key factor in how the Navy proceeds.

---

[55] Philip Ewing, "CNO: Navy Could've Been Clearer About LCS," *Politico Pro Defense*, May 21, 2014. Material in brackets as in original. See also Sandra Erwin, "Navy Chief: We Will Lay Out Clear Plan for Littoral Combat Ship," *National Defense (www.nationaldefensemagazine.org)*, May 21, 2014.

[56] Mike McCarthy, "Up-gunned LCSs, Coast Guard's Cutter Among Ideas Proposed For Navy's Small Surface Combatant," *Defense Daily*, May 23, 2014: 2-3.

"People who are thinking about doing something other than that (the current LCS) have to look at the price point that that ship is at," Hilarides told a group of reporters Thursday [May 29]. "The alternatives will need to be very close in price to where we currently are for it to be affordable."[57]

FY2015 LCS Program Funding Request

The Navy's proposed FY2015 budget requests $1,421.7 million in procurement funding for the procurement of three LCSs in FY2015, or an average of $475.7 million per ship, in the Shipbuilding and Conversion, Navy (SCN) appropriation account. The budget requests an additional $93.0 million in the SCN account to complete the costs of LCSs funded in prior years; this request forms part of a larger Navy request for $1,007.3 million in cost-to-complete funding for various Navy shipbuilding programs.

The Navy's proposed FY2015 budget also requests a total of $99.6 million in procurement funding for LCS mission modules in lines 34 through 37 of the Other Procurement, Navy (OPN) appropriation account.

Issues for Congress

Oversight Issues Arising from Request to Procure Three Rather Than Four LCSs in FY2015

The Navy's request in its proposed FY2015 budget for funding to procure three rather than four LCSs raises potential oversight questions for Congress, including the following:

- Why did the Navy decide to request funding for the procurement of three rather than four LCSs in FY2015?

- If three rather than four LCSs are funded in FY2015, which of the two LCS block buy contracts would not be fully implemented in its final year, and how would the Navy determine which contract would be the one to not be fully implemented?

- If three rather than four LCSs are funded in FY2015, what contractual arrangement would the Navy use to procure these LCSs?

- How would procuring three rather than four LCSs in FY2015 affect LCS unit procurement costs in FY2015 and subsequent years?

- How would procuring three rather than four LCSs in FY2015 affect the relative competitiveness of the two LCS builders for any competition the Navy might hold to determine who is to build LCSs procured in FY2016 and subsequent years?

---

[57] Mike McCarthy, "LCS Follow-On Will Have To Be 'Very Close' In Price, Admiral Says," *Defense Daily*, June 2, 1014: 4-5.

- The Navy has not yet announced an acquisition strategy for the LCSs to be procured in FY2016 and subsequent fiscal years that are needed to reach a total of 32 LCSs. In the absence of an announced acquisition strategy for those LCSs, how well can Congress consider whether it would make sense to procure three LCSs, four LCSs, or some other number of LCSs in FY2015?

Regarding the first three questions above, the Navy has testified that the Navy is requesting three rather than four LCSs for FY2015 because of constraints on the Navy's budget, and that if three LCSs are funded in FY2015, the Navy would seek to renegotiate one of the block buy contracts so that the fourth LCS that was previously planned for FY2015 would instead be procured in FY2016. At an April 10, 2014, hearing on Navy shipbuilding programs before the Seapower subcommittee of the Senate Armed Services Committee, Sean Stackley, the Assistant Secretary of the Navy for Research, Development, and Acquisition (i.e., the Navy's acquisition executive), testified that

> losing the last ship of the block- buy in [FY]'15 and moving into[FY]'16 was another one of the casualties of the drop in the [Department of the Navy's] budget. What we are going to do[—]we have not engaged in industry yet[—]is we're going to sit down with the two shipbuilders associated with the LCS program and we're going to look at production schedules, the vendor base and performance on the program and effectively look to extend the pricing—the pricing and validation date for that last ship between the two shipbuilders.
>
> In terms of what we anticipate as impact, I see zero impact in the shipyard based on the production schedules. The concern is the vendor base. So, we have to take a hard look at the sequence in which they're ordering material for that last ship and try to ensure that we don't incur—there will be some cost impact, this isn't going to go to zero but to minimize any cost impact associated with delays to ordering material.[58]

Regarding the fourth question above—How would procuring three rather than four LCSs in FY2015 affect LCS unit procurement costs in FY2015 and subsequent years?—the Navy's FY2014 budget submission projected a request for $1,824.9 million for four LCSs, or an average of $456.2 million per ship. The Navy's FY2015 budget submission requests $1,427.1 million for three LCSs, or an average of $475.7 million per ship. If two of the LCSs requested for procurement in FY2015 still have an average cost of about $456.2 million, then the cost of the third LCS requested for procurement in FY2015 would appear to have a procurement cost of about $514.7 million, or about $58.5 million (about 13%) more than projected under the FY2014 submission.

Oversight Issues Arising from DOD's February 24, 2014, Announcement

Hagel's February 24 announcement that "no new contract negotiations beyond 32 ships will go forward" and that the Navy is to submit "alternative proposals to procure a capable and lethal small surface combatant, generally consistent with the capabilities of a frigate" raises several potential oversight issues for Congress, including the Navy's plan for determining which of the

---

[58] Transcript of hearing. See also Olga Belogolova, "Navy To Meet With LCS Shipbuilders To Divvy Up Ship Buy in FY-15," *Inside the Navy*, April 14, 2014.

two LCS builders would receive one LCS in FY2015 rather than two, and the analytical basis for the actions affecting the LCS program announced by Hagel on February 24.

Potential Oversight Questions Relating to Figure of 32 Ships

Hagel's February 24 announcement that "no new contract negotiations beyond 32 ships will go forward" raises a number of potential oversight issues for Congress, including the following:

- The LCS program was created to address a validated requirement for the fleet to have additional capability for countering mines, small boats, and diesel submarines in littoral waters. Is this requirement still valid? If not, what operational analysis did DOD conduct to justify the revocation of this requirement?

- The Navy selected the LCS program as the most cost-effective program for filling the fleet's requirement for additional capability for countering mines, small boats, and diesel submarines in littoral waters. Has DOD conducted a formal analysis that demonstrates that there is a more cost-effective way to address these capability gaps?

- The Navy determined that a force of 52 LCSs (and 64 mission packages) is needed to provide the Navy with sufficient capacity for fully addressing the fleet's requirement for additional capability for countering mines, small boats, and diesel submarines in littoral waters. Has DOD conducted a formal analysis to show that the Navy now needs only 32 LCSs to provide sufficient capacity for fully addressing the fleet's requirements in these three mission areas? What are the potential operational implications of attempting to perform these missions with a Navy that includes 32 rather than 52 LCSs?

- Why did DOD settle on a figure of 32 ships, as opposed to some other number short of 52? What is DOD's analytical basis for the figure of 32?

- How would limiting the LCS program to 32 ships affect planned numbers of LCS mission packages?

- When does the Navy intend to announce an acquisition strategy for the LCSs that are to be procured in FY2016 and subsequent fiscal years that are needed to reach a total of 32 LCSs?

Potential Oversight Questions Relating to Follow-On Ship Generally Consistent With Capabilities of A Frigate

Hagel's February 24 announcement that the Navy is to submit "alternative proposals to procure a capable and lethal small surface combatant, generally consistent with the capabilities of a frigate" raises several potential oversight issues for Congress, including the following:

- Has DOD performed a new analysis of mission needs to identify what capability gaps the Navy might need to address through a new shipbuilding program? If not, then how can DOD know that it needs a new ship generally consistent with the capabilities of a frigate? Where is the properly validated requirement for such a ship?

- If DOD has performed a new analysis of mission needs, has it also performed a rigorous analysis of various possible approaches for meeting those mission needs—a study that might be known as an analysis of multiple concepts (AMC)—to show that a ship generally consistent with the capabilities of a frigate is not merely one way, but rather the best or most promising way, to meet those mission needs? If not, then how can DOD know that it needs a new ship generally consistent with the capabilities of a frigate?

- Prior to announcing the LCS program on November 1, 2001, the Navy did not perform a rigorous AMC to show that a ship like the LCS (i.e., a small, fast, modular combatant) was not merely one way, but rather the best or most promising way, to address the three capability gaps that the Navy had identified for countering mines, small boats, and diesel submarines in littoral waters. The lack of a pre-November 1, 2001, rigorous analysis focusing on these specific mission needs and showing that a ship like the LCS was the best or most promising approach for meeting them became an oversight issue for Congress on the LCS program, and later complicated the Navy's ability to defend the LCS program against criticisms of the program. Is DOD now proposing to go down a similar path on the ship that is to be generally consistent with the capabilities of a frigate? That is, is DOD in effect putting the cart before the horse by announcing a preferred solution (a ship generally consistent with the capabilities of a frigate) before it has rigorously defined the problem (mission needs and capability gaps) and explored all possible approaches for solving it? Is DOD's acquisition process being circumvented or short-circuited?

- If DOD has arrived at a preferred solution without having done a rigorous AMC, will Navy and DOD acquisition activities going forward "to set the ship up for the start of the acquisition process," as stated in the February 24, 2014, press report quoted above, be geared toward generating an after-the-fact justification for this solution? Is it still possible to contemplate an alternative approach of performing a rigorous AMC that allows for the possibility that some other approach (perhaps even a counter-intuitive one) might prove preferable? And if such a study were to conclude that a ship generally consistent with capabilities of a frigate is the best approach, will this result be tainted by the fact that it was conducted after the February 24, 2014, announcement? What affect might this situation have on the Navy's ability to defend this program years from now against criticisms that others might make against it?

- The LCS sea frame turned out to be much more expensive to procure than the Navy originally envisaged and advertised to Congress. How much risk is there that a new ship generally consistent with the capabilities of a frigate will prove to be considerably more expensive to procure than the Navy might currently envisage? If the ship were to turn out to be considerably more expensive to procure than currently envisaged, how might that affect DOD's judgment that a ship of this type represents the best path forward?

Generalized Arguments For and Against Truncating LCS Program

Supporters of truncating the LCS program to 32 ships or some other number well short of 52 could argue one or more of the following:

- **Alternative Potential Ways To Perform Missions.** There are alternative and potentially more cost effective ways to perform the LCSs' three primary missions of countering mines, small boats, and diesel-electric submarines, particularly in littoral waters. Possibilities include extending the service lives of existing mine warfare ships and mine warfare helicopters, equipping cruisers and destroyers (and their embarked helicopters and unmanned aerial vehicles) with small anti-ship weapons for countering small boats,[59] and using antisubmarine aircraft as well as attack submarines, cruisers, and destroyers (and their embarked helicopters and unmanned vehicles) to counter submarines.[60] The LCS's secondary missions could similarly be performed by other platforms, including Joint High Speed Vessels (JHSVs), amphibious ships, cruisers and destroyers, and attack submarines.

- **Procurement cost growth.** LCS sea frames have turned out to be much more expensive to procure than the original target of $220 million each in constant FY2005 dollars. This procurement cost growth makes the LCS program less cost effective than originally envisaged as a way of performing the program's three primary missions.

- **Potential O&S cost growth.** The possible increase in LCS core crew size that the Navy is considering would increase annual operating and support (O&S) costs for LCSs. Growth in LCS annual O&S costs would make the LCS program less cost effective than originally envisaged as a way of performing the program's three primary missions.

- **Potential cost of fixing design and construction issues.** The lead ships built to each LCS design have experienced a variety of design and construction issues. Fixing these issues on follow-on LCSs could make them more expensive to procure, which would make the LCS program less cost effective than originally envisaged as a way of performing the program's three primary missions.

- **Survivability of LCS design.** The LCS was designed to a Level I+ survivability standard, which is less than the Level II standard of the Navy's existing Oliver Hazard Perry (FFG-7) frigates, which are among the ships that LCSs effectively are to replace in the Navy's force structure.[61]

---

[59] The UK navy reportedly is using an approach broadly similar to this for countering swarm boats; see Richard Scott, "Protection From the Swarm," Jane's Defence Weekly, May 29, 2013: 24-28.

[60] Prior to announcing the LCS in November 2001, the Navy did not perform a formal study (which at the time might have been called an analysis of multiple concepts) to show through rigorous analysis that a small, fast, modular surface ship like the LCS was the most cost-effective way to perform the program's three primary missions. The Navy did not perform such a study until after the LCS program was announced; the results of this after-the-fact study could be tainted by the knowledge that the Navy had already announced the LCS program. For additional discussion, see, for example, pages 35-40 of the October 28, 2004, update of CRS Report RL32109, *Navy DDG-51 and DDG-1000 Destroyer Programs: Background and Issues for Congress*, by Ronald O'Rourke, *Navy DD(X) and LCS Ship Acquisition Programs: Oversight Issues and Options for Congress*, by Ronald O'Rourke, out of print and available directly from the author. (In 2004, CRS Report RL32109 covered both the DD(X) destroyer program—now called the DDG-1000 destroyer program—and the LCS program.)

[61] Navy surface ships traditionally have been designed to one of three survivability standards, called Level I (low), Level II (moderate), and Level II (high). Aircraft carriers, cruisers, and destroyers are designed to Level III. Frigates, amphibious ships, and certain underway replenishment (resupply) ships are designed to Level II. Other replenishment ships, as well as mine warfare ships, patrol craft, and support ships are designed to Level I. Although future Navy ships will be designed to a new set of survivability standards that the Navy recently established as a replacement for the (continued...)

- **Comparison with foreign frigates and corvettes.** In terms of amount of weaponry and other ship characteristics, the LCS does not fare well in comparisons with certain frigate and corvette designs operated by other navies.

- **Ability to perform missions.** A July 14, 2012, press report states that initial Navy experience with the lead LCSs has led to questions in the Navy about the prospective ability of LCSs to effectively perform certain missions.[62]

- **Changing mission priorities.** In the years that have passed since the LCS program was first announced in November 2001, countering China's maritime military modernization effort has become an increasing concern. Countering improved Chinese maritime military forces will involve procuring ships (such as destroyers and attack submarines) that are oriented toward ballistic missile defense, anti-ship cruise missile defense, countering larger surface ships, and countering submarines that are operating far from shore as well as in littoral waters.[63] The LCS is not optimized for most of these missions. The LCS's three primary missions of countering mines, small boats, and diesel-electric submarines, particularly in littoral waters, remain valid, but in a period of constrained defense spending, resources devoted to these missions must be balanced against resources devoted to ships with mission orientations that are more closely aligned with the goal of countering China's improving maritime military capabilities.

Opponents of truncating the LCS program to 32 ships or some other number well short of 52 could argue one or more of the following:

- **Alternative Potential Ways To Perform Missions.** Although there may be alternative potential ways to perform the LCSs' three primary missions of

---

(...continued)

Level I/II/III standards, the LCS and prior classes of warships will continue to be covered under the Level I/II/III standards.

The Navy plans to station up to eight LCSs at Bahrain, in the Persian Gulf. Currently, several Navy mine warfare ships and patrol craft are stationed at Bahrain, and the Navy regularly deploys other ships, including aircraft carriers, destroyers, frigates, and support ships, into the Gulf. In the late 1980s, two of the Navy's FFG-7 class frigates were severely damaged by enemy attack while operating in the Persian Gulf: In May 1987, the frigate Stark (FFG-31) was severely damaged by two Iraqi cruise missiles, and in April 1988 the frigate Samuel B. Roberts (FFG-58) was severely damaged by an Iranian mine. Both ships were saved by a combination of their built-in survivability features and the damage-control actions of their crews. (The ships were later repaired and returned to service.) How the physical structures of the two ships might have responded to the attacks if they had been designed to something less than a Level II survivability standard is not certain. Navy ships operating in the Gulf today continue to face significant potential threats from Iranian cruise missiles, mines, and other weapons. (See, for example, CRS Report R42335, *Iran's Threat to the Strait of Hormuz*, coordinated by Kenneth Katzman.)

[62] Christopher P. Cavas, "LCS: Quick Swap Concept Dead," *DefenseNews.com*, July 14, 2012. See also Christopher P. Cavas, "Maintenance Hurdles Mount for New USN Ship," *DefenseNews.com*, July 23, 2012; Michael Fabey, "U.S. Navy Finds More LCS-1 Issues During Special Trials," *Aerospace Daily & Defense Report*, June 21, 2012: 2; Christopher P. Cavas, "U.S. Navy's LCS Yet to Fulfill Its Promise," *DefenseNews.com*, April 15, 2012.

[63] In 2008-2009, the Navy reversed its plans for procuring larger surface combatants (i.e., destroyers) in response to changing mission priorities. As a result, the Navy truncated procurement of DDG-1000 destroyers, which were originally designed with an emphasis on land-attack and operations in littoral waters, and restarted procurement of DDG-51 destroyers, which the Navy judged to be more cost effective than a modified DDG-1000 would have been for BMD, area air defense, and blue-water ASW operations. For further discussion, see CRS Report RL32109, *Navy DDG-51 and DDG-1000 Destroyer Programs: Background and Issues for Congress*, by Ronald O'Rourke.

---

countering mines, small boats, and diesel-electric submarines, particularly in littoral waters, the LCS program was devised specifically to address these three capability gaps and remains the most economical way of addressing them. Critics of the LCS program cannot point to a rigorous study that shows a more cost effective way for performing these three primary missions. Extending the lives of existing mine warfare ships and mine warfare helicopters for more than a few years may not be feasible, and the LCS can perform the mission more effectively. Other types of ships, such as cruisers and destroyers, are already fully occupied performing their own missions; assigning LCS missions to these ships would reduce their capacity for performing their core missions.

- **Procurement cost growth.** Although LCS sea frames have turned out to be much more expensive to procure than the original target of $220 million each in constant FY2005 dollars, the LCS remains a relatively inexpensive surface combatant, and the program remains cost effective as a way of performing the program's three primary missions.

- **Potential O&S cost growth.** Although increasing the LCS core crew would increase annual operating and support (O&S) costs for LCSs, the increase would not be that great, and the program would remain cost effective as a way of performing the program's three primary missions.

- **Potential cost of fixing design and construction issues.** The lead ships in new Navy ship classes often experience design and construction issues. Fixing the LCSs' design and construction issues will not substantially increase the procurement cost of follow-on LCSs, and consequently will not make the program substantially less cost effective than originally envisaged as a way of performing the program's three primary missions.

- **Survivability of LCS design.** Although LCSs are not intended as direct replacements for the Navy's current patrol craft, mine warfare ships, and frigates, they are to perform missions that in several cases are similar to those currently performed by patrol craft, mine warfare ships, and frigates. The Navy decided to design the LCS to what it calls a Level 1+ survivability standard, which is greater than the Level I standard to which the Navy's current patrol craft and mine warfare ships were designed, and less than the Level II standard to which the Navy's current Oliver Hazard Perry (FFG-7) class frigates were designed. The Navy believes that, after taking planned ship employment and specific potential threats into proper account, a Level 1+ survivability standard is appropriate for the LCS.[64]

- **Comparison with foreign frigates and corvettes.** The LCS is by no means the only Navy surface combatant whose design has been initially criticized by some observers in terms of survivability, weaponry, or other design features. To the contrary, virtually every major class of U.S. Navy surface combatant built in recent decades was initially criticized by some observers on one ground or another, including the Knox (FF-1052) class frigates (of which 46 were

---

[64] See, for example, Michael Fabey, "LCS Council Chief Touts Ship Survivability Package," *Aerospace Daily & Defense Report*, March 29, 2013: 5; Mike McCarthy, "Navy Continues Defense of LCS Survivability," *Defense Daily*, January 17, 2013: 6-7.

eventually built), Oliver Hazard Perry (FFG-7) class frigates (of which 51 were eventually built), Spruance (DD-963) class destroyers (of which 31 were eventually built), Ticonderoga (CG-47) class Aegis cruisers (of which 27 were eventually built), and Arleigh Burke (DDG-51) class Aegis destroyers (of which 68 have been built or funded through FY2013, with additional ships requested or projected for FY2014 and subsequent fiscal years).[65] When assessed in terms of ability to perform the LCS program's three primary missions, the LCS fares well in terms of weaponry and other ship features in comparisons with frigate and corvette designs operated by other navies. The goal of the LCS program was not to design a small warship with as much onboard weaponry as possible (a goal that drives up procurement and operation and support costs), but rather to acquire a ship that could most cost effectively perform the program's three primary missions. The LCS is cost effective because it is designed to carry the equipment needed to perform its stated missions—nothing more and nothing less. Frigates and corvettes operated by other navies in general cannot perform at least one of the LCS's three primary missions, and in some cases are equipped with systems that are not needed to perform those missions.

- **Ability to perform missions.** The July 14, 2012, press report stating that initial Navy experience with the lead LCSs has led to questions in the Navy about the prospective ability of LCSs to effectively perform certain missions is based on a group of Navy studies and war games that were aimed at identifying what needs to be done to ensure that the LCS can perform its missions. The studies, in other words, were aimed at identifying problems, so that those problems could be fixed. Fixing these problems will ensure that the LCS will be able to perform its missions.[66]

- **Changing mission priorities.** Although countering China's maritime military modernization effort has become an increasing concern in recent years, Iran's littoral anti-access/area denial (A2/AD) capabilities (including small boats, mines, and diesel-electric submarines) remain a defense-planning concern. The LCS's ASW mission package will give the ship an ability to counter diesel-electric submarines far from shore, not just in littoral waters, and an ability to conduct ASW at higher speeds than other Navy surface combatants.[67] The Navy in recent years has also focused on missions such as peacetime engagement and partnership-building and maritime security and intercept (including anti-piracy operations)—missions that might be performed more cost effectively by LCSs than by cruisers and destroyers.

For some additional reference material relating to the question of whether to truncate the LCS program, see **Appendix E.**

---

[65] See, for example, Robert D. Holzer, "Birthing Ships Is Never Easy; Give LCS A Break," BreakingDefense.com, June 7, 2013, accessed July 22, 2013, at http://breakingdefense.com/2013/06/07/birthing-ships-is-never-easy-give-lcs-a-break/.

[66] Christopher P. Cavas, "LCS: Quick Swap Concept Dead," *DefenseNews.com*, July 14, 2012. See also Christopher P. Cavas, "Maintenance Hurdles Mount for New USN Ship," *DefenseNews.com*, July 23, 2012; Michael Fabey, "U.S. Navy Finds More LCS-1 Issues During Special Trials," *Aerospace Daily & Defense Report*, June 21, 2012: 2; Christopher P. Cavas, "U.S. Navy's LCS Yet to Fulfill Its Promise," *DefenseNews.com*, April 15, 2012.

[67] For an article discussing the latter point, see Michael Fabey, "Module To Make LCS A Faster Sub Hunter, Official Says," *Aerospace Daily & Defense Report*, April 9, 2013: 2.

Should There Be a Down Select to a Single LCS Design After the 24th Ship?

Another issue for Congress is whether there should be a down select to a single LCS design after the 24th ship (i.e., whether production of only one of the two designs should be continued upon completing the two block buy contracts in FY2015). The Navy's FY2013 30-year (FY2013-FY2042) shipbuilding plan, which was submitted to Congress on March 28, 2012 (i.e., when the Navy was still planning a force of 55 LCSs, as opposed to the subsequent planned total of 52), stated, "The DoN [Department of the Navy] will continue to procure both versions of the Littoral Combat Ship through FY2026 [i.e., through a total of 55 ships—the total number of LCSs planned at the time], and achieve the 55-ship inventory objective in FY2029."[68]

Supporters of down selecting to a single design after the 24th ship might argue that it would be uneconomical to continue production of two designs after FY2015 at the Navy's planned procurement rate of three ships per year (i.e., at a rate of 1.5 ships per year per shipyard). They might argue that maintaining ongoing competition between the two LCS builders through the end of the LCS program would not be critical, because the 2010 competition between the two LCS builders that resulted in the awarding of the two block buy contracts gave the Navy information on competitive pricing for LCSs, and because a down select competition between the two LCS builders in FY2016 would give the Navy additional information on competitive pricing for LCSs.

Opponents of down selecting to a single design after the 24th ship might argue that the Navy could maintain economical production at the planned rate of three ships per year by using ongoing competition between the two LCSs builders to award the third ship each year to the lower bidder. They might also argue that maintaining ongoing competition between the two LCS builders through the end of the LCS program would be critical for the Navy to generate bargaining leverage with the LCS builders in areas other than pricing, such as building ships on schedule, ensuring high construction quality, and developing innovations in processes that can further reduce production costs. They might also argue that it would be premature to down select to a single LCS design until the Navy knows what kind of ship it wants to build after 32 LCSs are funded, since that ship could be a variant of either LCS design and would most economically be produced by a warm production line.

Should Procurement of LCS Sea Frames and Mission Modules Be Slowed Until Operational Testing Is More Complete?

Another issue for Congress is whether procurement of LCS sea frames and mission modules should be slowed until operational testing of the sea frames and mission modules is more complete and other acquisition-process milestones are met. The issue arises from a July 2013 GAO report on the LCS program that states in its summary:

> The Littoral Combat Ship (LCS) seaframe program continues to face challenges stemming from concurrent design, production, and testing activities. The Navy has taken steps to resolve problems with the lead ships, and the shipyards are beginning to realize benefits from facility improvements and experience. However, testing remains to be completed and the

---

[68] U.S. Navy, *Annual Report to Congress on Long Range Plan for Construction of Naval Vessels for ⬚⬚⬚⬚*, April 2012, p. 16.

Navy is currently studying potentially significant design changes, such as increasing the commonality of systems between the two ship variants and changing ship capabilities. Changes at this point can compromise the positive impacts of shipyard learning, increase costs, and prolong schedules. The mission module program also has concurrency issues, and testing to date has shown considerable limitations in capabilities. The Navy is pursuing an incremental approach to fielding mission packages, but it has yet to finalize the requirements for each increment and does not plan to achieve the minimum performance requirements for the mine countermeasures and surface warfare packages until the final increments are fielded in 2017 and 2019, respectively.

The Navy continues to buy LCS seaframes and modules even as significant questions remain about the program and its underlying business case. Elements of the LCS business case, including its cost, the time needed to develop and field the system, and its anticipated capabilities have degraded over time. There are also significant unknowns related to key LCS operations and support concepts and the relative advantages and disadvantages of the two seaframe variants. The potential effect of these unknowns on the program is compounded by the Navy's aggressive acquisition strategy. By the time key tests of integrated LCS capability are completed in several years, the Navy will have procured or have under contract more than half of the planned number of seaframes. Almost half of the planned seaframes are already under contract, and the Navy plans to award further contracts in 2016, before the Department of Defense (DOD) makes a decision about full rate production of the ships. The Navy will not be able to demonstrate that mission packages integrated with the seaframes can meet the minimum performance requirements until operational testing for both variants (Freedom and Independence) is completed, currently planned for 2019.

The Navy has also essentially bypassed two major acquisition reviews for mission modules, purchasing 8 of the 64 planned mission packages before gaining approval to enter the system development and initial production phases.[69]

In a section on "Matters for Congressional Consideration," the report states:

1. To ensure that the Navy has adequate knowledge to support moving forward with future seaframe construction, Congress should consider restricting future funding to the program for construction of additional seaframes until the Navy:

  • completes the ongoing LCS technical and design studies,

  • determines the impacts of making any changes resulting from these studies on the cost and designs of future LCS seaframes, and

  • reports to Congress on cost-benefit analyses of changes to the seaframes to change requirements and/or capabilities and to improve commonality of systems, and the Navy's plan moving forward to improve commonality.

2. To ensure that information on the relative capabilities of each seaframe variant is communicated in a timely and complete manner, Congress should consider requiring DOD to report on the relative advantages of each variant in carrying out the three primary LCS

---

[69] Government Accountability Office, *Navy Ship Building Significant Investments in the Littoral Combat Ship Continue Amid Substantial Unknowns about Capabilities Use and Cost*, GAO-13-530, July 2013, summary page.

missions. This report should be submitted to Congress prior to the planned full-rate production decision and the award of any additional seaframe contracts.[70]

In a section on "Recommendations for Executive Action," the report states:

> To ensure that, going forward, relevant oversight entities are able to provide appropriate decision-makers with additional insight into future contract awards for seaframes, we recommend that the Secretary of the Defense direct the Secretary of the Navy to take the following two actions:
>
> 1. If the Navy is approved by USD AT&L to award additional seaframe block buy contracts for LCS 25 and beyond, ensure that it only procures the minimum quantity and rate of ships required to preserve the mobilization of the production base until the successful completion of the full-rate production decision review. The award of any additional seaframe contracts should be informed by
>
> • a new independent cost estimate conducted by DOD's Cost Assessment and Program Evaluation office, and
>
> • a re-validated capabilities development document.
>
> 2. Prior to the full-rate production decision and the award of any additional seaframe contracts, report to Congress on the relative advantages of each seaframe variant for each of the three mission areas.
>
> To facilitate mission module development and ensure that the Navy has adequate knowledge to support further module purchases, we recommend that the Secretary of the Defense direct the Secretary of the Navy to take the following two actions:
>
> 3. Ensure that the Acquisition Program Baseline submitted for the mission modules Milestone B establishes program goals—thresholds and objectives—for cost, schedule, and performance for each increment per current DOD acquisition policy.
>
> 4. To ensure that the purchase of mission modules do not outpace key milestones, buy only the minimum quantities of mission module systems required to support operational testing.[71]

The GAO report is listed on the GAO website with a date of July 22, 2013. The report was effectively released on July 25, 2013, concurrent with a hearing that day on the LCS program before the Seapower and Projection Forces subcommittee of the House Armed Services Committee that focused on the GAO report and featured witnesses from GAO and the Navy.

GAO's prepared statement for the hearing was based on the GAO report.[72] GAO's witness—Paul L. Francis, Managing Director Acquisition and Sourcing Management—recommended that DOD

---

[70] Government Accountability Office, *Na□y □□ip□□il□in□□□□□□nificant □n□estments in t□e □ittoral □om□at □□ip □ontin□e Ami□ □□□stantial □n□nowns a□o□t □apa□ilities□□se □an□ □ost*, GAO-13-530, July 2013, p. 55.

[71] Government Accountability Office, *Na□y □□ip□□il□in□□□□□□nificant □n□estments in t□e □ittoral □om□at □□ip □ontin□e Ami□ □□□stantial □n□nowns a□o□t □apa□ilities□□se □an□ □ost*, GAO-13-530, July 2013, p. 56.

[72] Navy Shipbuilding[:] Significant Investments in the Littoral Combat Ship Continue Amid Substantial Unknowns about Capabilities, Use, and Cost, Statement of Paul L. Francis, Managing Director Acquisition and Sourcing Management, Testimony Before the Subcommittee on Seapower and Projection Forces, Committee on Armed Services, House of Representatives, July 25, 2013, 8 pp.

---

limit future LCS seaframe acquisitions until DOD completes a full-rate production review, and that the Navy limit LCS mission module purchases to the minimum quantities required to support operational testing. In making this recommendation, Francis drew upon points made in the GAO report, including those reprinted above.[73]

The Navy's witnesses at the hearing—Sean Stackley, the Assistant Secretary of the Navy for Research, Development, and Acquisition (i.e., the Navy's acquisition executive), and Vice Admiral Richard Hunt, Director, Navy Staff, and the head of the Navy's LCS Council—acknowledged that the LCS program was started poorly in terms of acquisition approach and management, but argued that the program was subsequently restructured and is now a model of acquisition best practices. They stated that the Navy will keep Congress and GAO fully informed about the program. They opposed the idea of slowing or pausing procurement of LCS sea frames or mission modules on the grounds that doing so would delay the delivery of needed capabilities to the fleet, slow the growth of the Navy toward its goal of a 306-ship fleet, and increase LCS procurement costs by interrupting the block buy contracts, breaking production learning curves, and destabilizing work forces at the LCS shipyards and supplier firms. They argued that the initial increments of the mission modules pose little technical risk, since they rely on existing systems rather than new-development systems, and that the biggest challenge to the testing of the mission modules at this point relates to program stops and restarts caused by funding instability as a consequence of continuing resolutions, sequestration, and congressional marks and rescissions. They argued that the initial increments of the mission modules have already demonstrated capability equal to or greater than that of analogous systems on the existing ships that LCSs are effectively to replace (i.e., the Navy's Avenger (MCM-1) class mine warfare ships, Cyclone (PC-1) class patrol craft, and Oliver Hazard Perry (FFG-7) class frigates).[74] The Navy's prepared statement for the hearing states:

---

[73] Transcript of hearing.

[74] Source: Transcript of hearing. Regarding MCM capability, the Navy states elsewhere that "Increment I of the [LCS] MCM MP [mission package] will exceed the sustained area coverage rate of the Avenger Class [MCM] ship by approximately two times, based on developmental testing conducted to date and initial analysis." More fully, the Navy states the following regarding the LCS's MCM capability compared to that of the Navy's existing Avenger-class MCM ships:

> There are two significant advantages that the Littoral Combat Ship (LCS) with a Mine Countermeasures Mission Package (MCM MP) has over the Navy's current MCM Avenger Class [MCM] ship: removing the ship from the minefield and the increased speed of MCM operations. In accordance with the LCS MCM MP's concept of operations, the ship is removed from the minefield by relying on off-board, unmanned systems, instead of ship-mounted systems. This avoids the risk associated with exposing the manned Avenger Class ship and its crew of approximately 80 to mines. The use of unmanned systems also enables minehunting at much higher speeds than the legacy systems can achieve. MCM MP Increment I provides rapid, sustained minehunting, and clearance capabilities with the MH60-S Helicopter, the Remote Multi-Mission Vehicle (RMMV), the AQS-20A minehunting sonar, the Airborne Mine Neutralization System (AMNS), and the Airborne Laser Mine Detection System (ALMDS). Increment I of the [LCS] MCM MP will exceed the sustained area coverage rate of the Avenger Class [MCM] ship by approximately two times, based on developmental testing conducted to date and initial analysis.

> This analysis is based on the Naval Mine Warfare Simulation (NMWS) model and reflects a 95% confidence level achieved through Monte Carlo simulation. The NMWS model includes ship and system performance parameters such as, system launch, handling and recovery time, sensor swath width, maintenance delays, etc. The input loaded into the NMWS model for each performance parameter is based on measured system level activities performed on LCS during developmental testing. The NMWS model was initially accredited in 2004 and is regularly updated with real-life data collected during integration and at-sea developmental testing conducted to date. Additional independent analysis was conducted by Metron at the request of OPNAV in 2010 to validate the

(continued...)

The entire LCS program, as defined by the Joint Requirements Oversight Council (JROC)-approved LCS Flight 0+ Capability Development Document (CDD), defines the ends state requirements for the mission package increments as well as the requirements for the seaframe. Both seaframe variants are designed to meet the CDD specified requirements and support all three types of mission packages. Each variant is built to be compliant with the LCS Interface Control Document (ICD), which governs the interface between the ship and any current or future mission package. This incremental approach minimizes concurrency risk while allowing the flexibility which the modular concept provides. The nine mission package "increments" (4 MCM, 4 SUW, 1 ASW) represent time-phased fielding of capability aboard both variants of LCS seaframes. This time phased-fielding of capability is fundamental as it allows the Navy to rapidly field systems as they are matured instead of waiting for the final capability delivery. The major systems that comprise mission packages are already established as individual programs, with their own Acquisition Program Baselines (APBs) including cost, schedule and performance objectives and thresholds. One APB for the entire mission package program, which integrates these programs for LCS, is appropriate and compliant with law, regulation, and policy. The APB will include well-defined, quantitative cost, schedule and performance thresholds and objectives for the mission packages. In accordance with the CDD and the incremental approach, these targets will be met through the final, time-phased capabilities fielded for the MCM, SUW, and ASW mission packages. This is similar to the approach used for other programs which provide time-phased capability for platforms. The time-phased fielding of capability and the associated performance metrics to conduct testing against will be defined in the Capability Production Documents currently under development for each mission package.

Future seaframe contract awards will be predicated on meeting seaframe requirements, including the requirement to embark any ICD compliant mission package, in the most cost effective way. As the Navy prepares for the next procurement of ships, developmental and operational testing of the capabilities of each seaframe variant and associated mission package is being conducted and the results will be used to inform future program decisions. In addition, the Navy will have return cost data from the initial ships of the block buy to further inform the Fiscal Year (FY) 2016 procurement. The Defense Acquisition Board, chaired by USD(AT&L), will review the next seaframe procurement prior to Request for Proposal (RFP) release. The Navy, in conjunction with USD(AT&L), will execute the

---

(...continued)

NMWS model inputs/outputs.

The Navy is executing an incremental acquisition approach that adds capability to the mission packages as technologies mature. Through this incremental approach, the program will add a beach zone mine detection capability in Increment II (FY15) with the COBRA system on a Firescout Unmanned Air Vehicle; a mine sweeping and a near-surface neutralization capability in Increment III (FY17) with the Unmanned Influence Sweep System (UISS) and an upgrade to the AMNS; and finally, buried mine and surf-zone mine detection capabilities in Increment IV (FY19) with the Knifefish Unmanned Underwater Vehicle (UUV) and an upgrade to the COBRA system. Increment IV represents the baseline capability for the MCM MP as defined in the LCS Flight 0+ Capability Development Document (CDD). The Navy projects the baseline configuration of the MCM MP to exceed approximately four times the sustained area coverage rate of the Avenger class ship and its legacy systems.

The Navy is currently in the process of documenting the incremental performance requirements for each increment in Capability Production Documents (CPDs). The performance of the MCM MP at each increment will be documented in a CPD. The performance expectations derived from the NMWS model and insights from developmental testing will be incorporated into the incremental plan to achieve required performance.

(Navy information paper on LCS program dated August 26, 2013, and provided to CRS and CBO on August 29, 2013.)

---

normal, rigorous process to ensure that the procurement meets with the specified requirements and that the costs are well understood. As the Navy continues to build LCS seaframes, the LCS mission package procurements are phased to meet the number of LCS Seaframes. To keep pace with the LCS seaframes currently under contract or remaining under the current block buy through Fiscal Year (FY) 2015, the Navy must procure mission package at a rate necessary to support, 1) developmental and initial operational test and evaluation of the two LCS variants, 2) developmental and operational testing of each incremental mission package capability as it is integrated and fielded, 3) Fleet crew training needs, and 4) operational LCS units with the tailored capabilities required for seaframe deployments. It is important to note that it is not a one-to-one ratio of mission package to LCS Seaframes. In FY 2014 for example, there will be four seaframes delivered to the fleet with a total of 10 mission packages (5 MCM and 5 SUW) delivered and available for use. The additional mission packages will support not only operational deployments, but account for the additional needs of training, and maintenance as well as developmental and operational testing....

The Navy plans to procure LCS seaframes in accordance with the most recent long range shipbuilding plan while balancing available funding with achieving the lowest possible pricing to the government. The future acquisition decisions will be informed with an up-to-date Service Cost Position and "should cost" assessment. The Defense Acquisition Executive will determine whether a new OSD Cost Analysis and Program Evaluation (CAPE) Independent Cost Estimate (ICE) will be needed to inform the decision. Contracts for ships in FY 2016 and beyond will be informed by actual cost returns, not estimates, for eight delivered seaframes and an additional 16 seaframes under contract, but not delivered by FY 2016. The Joint Staff, along with the Navy staff, plans to conduct a requirements assessment study which will serve as a revalidation of the LCS capabilities definition document. No changes to LCS seaframe requirements are envisioned in the near term as both LCS classes meet Navy requirements. No changes are planned for LCS mission packages that will affect near-term testing or fielding of mission package systems.[75]

---

[75] Statement of the Honorable Sean J. Stackley, Assistant Secretary of the navy (Research, Development and Acquisition), and Vice Admiral Richard Hunt, Director, Navy Staff, Before the Subcommittee on Seapower & Projection Forces of the House Armed Services Committee on Department of the Navy Shipbuilding Programs, July 25, 2013, pp. 3-4 and 12. For press accounts of the July 25, 2013, see, for example, Christopher P. Cavas, "LCS Hearing Attracts A Packed House, But Comity Breaks Out," *DefenseNews.com*, July 25, 2013; Andrea Shalal-Esa, "U.S. Navy Defends New Warship, Warns Against Slowing Production," *Reuters.com*, July 25, 2013; Emelie Rutherford, "Panel Pledges Close LCS Oversight," *Defense Daily*, July 26, 2013: 1; Michael Fabey, "Congress To Decide If LCS Is Worth The Risk," *Aerospace Daily & Defense Report*, July 26, 2013: 1.

Opponents of slowing or pausing LCS procurement might also argue the following:

- The current situation of LCS sea frames and mission modules being procured ahead of operational testing and other acquisition milestones is a natural and expected consequence of the program's initial rapid acquisition strategy and the award of the two block buy contracts, both of which Congress reviewed and approved. Congress' decision to approve the award of the two block buy contracts followed a December 14, 2010, hearing before the Senate Armed Services Committee that specifically reviewed the pros and cons of the Navy's proposal to award the two block buy contracts, with testimony from the Navy, GAO, CBO, and CRS (see **Appendix D**).

- There is nothing amiss in the fact that the Navy is considering potential design changes to the LCS—the Navy often does this in shipbuilding programs that are expected to have long production runs. In recent years, for example, the Navy considered and then implemented design changes during the production runs of the Ticonderoga (CG-47) class Aegis cruisers, the Arleigh Burke (DDG-51) class Aegis destroyers, and the Los Angeles (SSN-688) class attack submarines, and is doing the same today in the DDG-51 program and the Virginia (SSN-774) class attack submarine program. Design changes in a ship class with a long production run can result from the emergence of new technologies or a desire to modify a ship's capabilities in response to changing operational needs. In light of the long production run anticipated for the LCS, it would be surprising—and arguably troubling—if the Navy were not considering potential design changes for the LCS.

Technical Risk in LCS Program

Another potential oversight issue for Congress concerns the amount of technical risk in the LCS program. The discussion below addresses this issue first with respect to the LCS sea frame, and then with respect to LCS mission packages.

Sea Frame

March 2014 GAO Report

A March 2014 GAO report assessing DOD weapon acquisition programs stated:

Technology Maturity

Sixteen of the 18 critical technologies for both LCS designs are mature and have been demonstrated in a realistic environment. The two remaining technologies—LCS 1's overhead launch and retrieval system and LCS 2's aluminum structure are nearing maturity—according to our best practice standards. Though program officials believe that LCS 2's aluminum structure hull is mature as the ship is operational, there are still unknowns related to the hull structure. As a result, full maturity will not be demonstrated until the completion of shock and survivability trials to validate survivability and the ship's ability to achieve a 20-year service life. These tests are not expected to begin until August 2015.

Design and Production Maturity

The Navy started construction of LCS 1 and 2 without a stable design and has had to incorporate design changes on follow-on seaframes. LCS 1 and LCS 2 are still undergoing testing, and the Navy is incorporating design fixes for identified deficiencies into the designs of follow-on ships. In addition, a series of additional design changes for both variants have been approved by the LCS Council for fiscal year 2015; including bridge wings and a seven-meter rigid hull inflatable boat for the Independence variant and stronger stern ramp for the Freedom variant. LCS 4 experienced delays and was delivered six months after its expected contract delivery date of March 2013. LCS 5 through LCS 12 are currently in various stages of construction. The Navy is concerned about both contractors' ability to meet construction schedules without impacting follow-on hulls.

LCS 1 completed a ten-month deployment to the western pacific in December 2013 where it operated out of Singapore. During this deployment it encountered two significant engineering issues that significantly curtailed its ability to get underway: the lubrication cooling system ruptured and the ship service diesel engine generator had reliability issues. In addition to these engineering issues, LCS 1 had a number of combat system and other material failures; including radar underperformance and the combat system unexpectedly rebooting during operations.

Other Program Issues

The Navy added 20 permanent berths to LCS 1 to support additional manning for its deployment to Singapore in 2013. In May 2013, the Navy determined that additional permanent accommodations for a total crew size of 98 should be incorporated in all LCS class ships. The LCS program executive office has been directed to add these permanent accommodations through either forward -or back-fitting the ships. Although the habitability modification installed on LCS 1 in support of its deployment did not include the addition of increased storage and water supplies, the forward fit installs will address the required services and auxiliary system modifications associated with the installation of the additional berthing. Following LCS 1's 2013 deployment, the Navy will evaluate lessons learned and future manning options. The Navy expects to complete this evaluation in fiscal year 2014 and incorporate any proposed manning changes beginning in fiscal year 2015 ahead of the next block buy decision in 2016, when 24 seaframes will already be delivered, constructed, or under contract.

Program Office Comments

In commenting on a draft of this assessment, the program office noted that LCS 4 showed significant improvement from LCS 2 in level of completeness and number of high priority trial cards deficiencies at delivery. Twelve block buy ships are funded on the block buy contract and are in pre-production or construction, following thorough production readiness reviews. LCS 5 and 6 launched in December 2013. LCS 1 deployment successfully validated major portions of the LCS concept of operations for crew rotation and contracted overseas maintenance. Ship service diesel generator and seawater cooler reliability issues were satisfactorily addressed during deployment. Engineering changes have been incorporated to prevent and mitigate those issues in the future. Material failures of the radar were a result of a procedural error causing the system to reboot, however the radar performed to design specifications. The program office also provided technical comments, which were incorporated where deemed appropriate.[76]

January 2014 DOT&E Report

Regarding technical risk in the LCS sea frame, a January 2014 report from DOD's Director, Operational Test and Evaluation (DOT&E)—DOT&E's annual report for FY2013—states:

Seaframes

• While both seaframe variants are fast and highly maneuverable, they are lightly armed for ships of this size and possess no significant offensive capability without the planned SUW Increment IV mission package.

- They have very modest self-defense capabilities; their air defense capabilities cannot be characterized fully until tests on LCS 5 and LCS 6 (the production-representative seaframes) and the Navy's unmanned Self-Defense Test Ship feed the Navy Probability of Raid Annihilation high-fidelity modeling and simulation analyses in FY18.

- The surface self-defense capability is scheduled to undergo limited testing in the first OT&E events on LCS 2 and LCS 3 in FY14, but the Navy has deferred testing of the ships' capability to defeat unmanned aerial vehicles and slow-flying aircraft until production-representative seaframes are available.

- The seaframes have no systems designed to detect torpedo attacks or mines without the appropriately configured mission packages installed.

---

[76] Government Accountability Office, *Defense Acquisitions—Assessments of Selected Weapon Programs*, GAO-14-340SP, March 2014, p. 94.

• Results from the QRA [Quick Reaction Assessment] revealed performance, reliability, and operator training deficiencies for the 57 mm gun on LCS 1 that prevented the ship from demonstrating it can meet the Navy's SUW performance requirements.

- The Navy reported that the observed deficiencies have been corrected on LCS 1; and that those corrections were satisfactorily demonstrated during developmental testing in October 2012; however, no data were collected during that testing to facilitate an independent assessment.

- The preliminary analysis of data collected during recent testing of the 57 mm gun conducted on LCS 3 in October 2013, which was observed by DOT&E, indicates that the gun reliability has improved. DOT&E expects to issue a formal test report in 4QFY14 after the Navy has completed IOT&E of the Freedom variant seaframe and Increment II SUW mission package.

• Crew size can limit the mission capabilities and combat endurance of the ship. The Navy continues to review manning to determine appropriate levels. The Navy installed 20 additional berths in LCS 1 for flexibility during its deployment and has stated that additional berths will be installed in all seaframes.

• Freedom Variant (LCS 1 and 3):

- Developmental testing demonstrated that this variant can position, launch, and recover the 11-meter boats included in the SUW mission package as long as the launch, recovery, and handling system is operational. Replacement of the aluminum launch ramp with one constructed of steel allows a boat to be stored on the ramp to reduce the launch time and improve responsiveness. The Navy has not tested the ship's capability to handle, launch, and recover other watercraft.

- COMBATSS-21 [combat system] and TRS-3D [radar] performance deficiencies have affected target detection and tracking capabilities in developmental testing.

- The QRA performed by COTF [Commander, Operartional Test and Evaluation Force] uncovered vulnerabilities in the ship's capability to protect the security of information.

- Failures of diesel-powered generators, air compressors, and propulsion drive train components have degraded the seaframe's operational availability. The Navy reports that recent reliability improvements made to the affected seaframe components have led to improved operational availability of the seaframe; however, no formal developmental or operational testing has occurred to quantify that improvement.

• Independence Variant (LCS 2):

- DOT&E has no data to assess the core mission capabilities of the Independence variant seaframe.

- The Independence crew encountered multiple problems with the twin-boom extensible crane (TBEC) and other mission package support systems during initial developmental testing of the MCM mission package. Since then, the vendor improved the TBEC and the Navy made RMMV [Remote Multi-Mission Vehicle] hardware changes. Developmental testing in August 2013 demonstrated the ship's capability to launch and recover the RMMV has improved.

- Availability of the Independence to support testing has been degraded by equipment failures, including problems with operator consoles, power generation equipment, components of the ship's computing and networking equipment, propulsion drive train components, and communications systems. The Navy reports that recent reliability improvements made to the affected seaframe components have led to improved operational availability of the Independence; however, no formal developmental or operational testing has occurred to quantify that improvement....

LFT&E [Live Fire Test and Evaluation]

• The initial aluminum fire testing focused on the strength degradation of aluminum panels and welds at elevated temperatures. Follow-on testing in FY14 will investigate structural collapse of a multi-compartment aluminum structure due to fire exposure. The tearing tests collected data needed to develop methodologies suitable for the simulation of ductile fracture on the structural scale within the framework of whole-ship finite element analyses. Data analysis continues; the Detail Design Survivability Assessment Report is scheduled to complete in FY16.

• LCS is not expected to be survivable in high-intensity combat because the design requirements do not require the inclusion of survivability features necessary to conduct sustained combat operations in a major conflict as expected for the Navy's other surface combatants.[77]

November 15, 2013, Press Report on a Classified GAO Report

A November 15, 2013, press report stated:

> The Littoral Combat Ship (LCS) fleet has some communication problems that need to be addressed to enable the vessels to operate as planned, a recent U.S. Government Accountability Office (GAO) report says, and Navy officials say they are assessing the problems and GAO recommendations.
>
> "The Navy identified limitations in its four internal reports with LCS communications systems' ability to transmit data electronically," GAO says in a recent for-official-use-only report, "Littoral Combat Ship, Navy Needs to Address Communication System Limitations and Obtain Additional Operational and Cost Data." The report is not available publicly.
>
> "LCS depends on operational and maintenance support from the shore more than other Navy ships, so reliability and adequacy of communication systems, and the bandwidth required to transmit information, are critical to effective operations and sustainment," GAO notes.
>
> "As with all of our new ship classes, a lot of effort is made in evaluating how to improve the Littoral Combat Ship," spokeswoman Lt. Caroline Hutcheson says. "Recommendations from the organizations like GAO and its report have been part of detailed discussions as the Navy assesses the program. The LCS Council is addressing the ships' communications systems... ." The Lockheed Martin-built LCS-1, the USS Freedom, is on deployment in Singapore. Hutcheson says there has been no significant operational impact for Freedom on deployment due to the communications issue....
>
> "LCS relies on the Navy Information Application Product Suite system to transmit data, using bandwidth capacity to do so, as do many of the distance support functions," the report

---

[77] Department of Defense, Director, Operational Test & Evaluation, *Annual Report*, January 2014, pp. 198-199, 200.

says. "One internal Navy report found that problems with the system led to sensor data not leaving the ships for months, among other connectivity issues."

The Navy internal report's finding that "the LCS concept depends on distance support of ships, but the [information technology] pipes to make it happen aren't reliable yet" led to a recommendation to "accelerate implementation of the condition-based maintenance program," GAO says....

"The Navy Information Application Product Suite system used by LCS was not originally designed to support the continuous flow of LCS data," GAO says. "Because LCS depends heavily on distance support and especially applications based on this system, the Navy recognizes that alternative communication methods are necessary to ensure that the flow of information to shore is not interrupted in the event of an extended loss of capabilities, particularly during wartime."

Navy officials told GAO existing communication systems are being "adapted for use on LCS but are not ideal for the unique needs of the ship even though the systems meet program requirements."[78]

Mission Packages

March 2014 GAO Report

The March 2014 GAO report assessing DOD weapon acquisition programs stated:

Mine Countermeasures (MCM)

The Navy has accepted four packages without demonstrating that they meet requirements and plans to accept two more in fiscal 2014. The package will be fielded in four increments: the first intends to remove sailors from the minefield and improve mine detection, classification, and destruction over legacy vessels. Although DOD states that all systems in increment one are fully mature, developmental testing has shown performance problems that led to changes in planned tactics, removal of systems, and lowered testing requirements. For example, corrections to the mine-hunting sonar's reliability have yet to be validated in operational testing, and two systems, intended to sweep for and neutralize mines, had to be removed for safety and performance issues. Also, the Navy now requires multiple searches to identify mines, adding time to the process, and has lowered increment one testing requirements for mine clearance rates. If operational testing proves successful, this package will not be able to replace all legacy capability until increment three completion in fiscal 2017.

Surface Warfare (SUW)

The Navy has taken delivery of four packages, each comprised of two 30 millimeter guns, as well as a rigid hull inflatable boat prototype, boarding gear, and armed helicopters. Following the cancellation of the non-line-of-sight launch system, the Navy planned to field the Griffin missile in 2015 as an initial capability. However, program officials stated that the Navy is rethinking this and a solution is not yet known.

---

[78] Michael Fabey, "Report Cites LCS Communications Problems," *Aerospace Daily & Defense Report* (*www.aviationweek.com*), November 15, 2013. See also Tony Capaccio, "Littoral Ship-to-Shore Comunications Seen Deficient, GAO Says," *Bloomberg News*, November 19, 2013.

Antisubmarine Warfare (ASW)

The Navy restarted development of an ASW package with new requirements as the initial package was not going to deliver enough capability over legacy assets. The Navy is assessing a replacement, with initial delivery planned in 2016, that is expected to include, among other technologies, a variable-depth sonar—which, according to officials, performed well in initial tests—and a towed array. The maturity of these technologies has not yet been independently assessed.

Other Program Issues

The Navy held a preliminary design review in 2004, but the packages have substantively changed. The program held a milestone B event in January 2014 with an estimated acquisition cost of $7.24 billion. Tests for increment one and two of the SUW and increment one of the MCM package are scheduled for fiscal 2014 and 2015 respectively. These assessments evaluate progress in achieving baseline performance capability, which includes all planned increments for each package. The Navy plans to purchase 32 LCS seaframes and take delivery of at least 24 by the time the baseline performance capabilities of the MCM and SUW packages are proven and fielded.

Program Office Comments

The Navy states that our assessment of program cost growth incorrectly compares the acquisition program baseline against a fiscal 2008 baseline, which does not reflect the total acquisition. Further, the Navy states that this assessment disregards near term operational requirements as the data presented indicates that the program should be delayed. The Navy also states that our assertion of excessive program risk, due to concurrency, is unfounded because developmental testing, combined with capability proven during early deployments, has significantly reduced technical risk. This is evidence, according to the Navy, that the LCS will successfully complete operational testing. Lastly, the current missile procurement was delayed due to sequestration; the Navy states that the program is on track to deliver a capability in late 2016.

GAO Response

In comparing the 2007 estimate with the acquisition program baseline, we used the Navy's 2007 data, which included full procurement costs but only five years of development cost. The Navy has acquired eight packages without proving capability through operational testing. In the absence of a defined increment-based approach for the full baseline capability to sequentially gain knowledge and meet these requirements, the Navy's acquisition approach is not in accordance with best practices or DOD guidance in place at the time of our review.[79]

January 2014 DOT&E Report

Regarding technical risk in LCS mission packages, the January 2014 DOT&E report states:

SUW Mission Package

---

[79] Government Accountability Office, *Defense Ac□isitions□□□Assessments of □electe□ □eapon □ro□rams*, GAO-14-340SP, March 2013, p. 96.

• Results from the QRA [Quick Reaction Assessment] revealed performance, reliability, and operator training deficiencies for both the 30 mm guns that prevented the ship from demonstrating that it can meet the Navy's SUW performance requirements. However, as installed in the Freedom variant, the Increment II SUW mission package does enhance existing surface self-defense capability and provides additional capability to conduct maritime interdiction operations; it has not been tested in the Independence variant seaframe.

MCM Mission Package

• The Navy has not yet demonstrated the interim sustained area coverage rate requirement through end-to-end testing. Developmental testing has focused primarily on integrating the Increment I MCM mission package on the Independence. The MCM mission package has not been tested with the Freedom variant seaframe.

• During operational assessments completed in 2011 and 2012, the AN/AQS-20A [sonar] and ALMDS [airborne laser mine detection system] systems that compose the Increment I minehunting sensors demonstrated some capability in favorable benign operating environments, but failed to meet all performance requirements established by the Navy.

- AN/AQS-20A contact depth localization errors in all operating modes and false contacts in two of the three search modes exceeded Navy limits. ALMDS failed to achieve the desired detection performance over the depth range prescribed by the Navy and the system's false contacts exceeded Navy limits by a wide margin.

- While the Navy has identified mitigations for some of these deficiencies, they require additional search missions to weed out most of the false contacts. The additional search missions will reduce LCS's search rate.

- Data from these operational assessments also bring into question the ability of the two minehunting systems to search the full water column; the Navy is conducting additional tests to determine if there are gaps in coverage. The Navy is also developing an improved version of the AN/AQS-20A and expects to begin developmental testing in FY14.

• AMNS, intended to provide identification and neutralization of in-volume and bottom mines, will provide the only mine neutralization capability in the Increment I MCM mission package.

- Since the Navy has stopped the development of the Rapid Airborne Mine Clearance System (RAMICS), Increment I will not provide near-surface mine neutralization capability.

- The operational assessment that the Navy planned to conduct in FY13 has slipped to FY14.

- The Navy plans to develop an improved version of AMNS that will include the capability to neutralize near-surface mines; however, that development is not currently funded. The Navy expects AMNS to achieve initial operating capability (IOC) in FY16.

• The RMS [remote mine-hunting system], which is critical to achieving the Navy's sustained area coverage rate requirement, has also experienced developmental delays.

- The Navy expects RMS to achieve IOC in 4QFY15 [the fourth quarter of FY2015]. Contractor tests completed in FY13 suggest that RMMV reliability has grown since the RMS program emerged from the Nunn-McCurdy review in FY10; however, these tests were not conducted in an operationally realistic manner and the measure used was not operationally relevant resulting in artificially high estimates of reliability. Data from the recent development testing suggest that reliability may not have improved sufficiently to enable an

LCS with two RMMVs onboard to complete the desired area search without having to return to port more often than currently planned and desired to obtain replacements. An accurate quantitative assessment of achieved RMMV reliability cannot be evaluated until the RMS is tested in operationally realistic minehunting missions (test conditions not achieved during the contractor testing).

- The analysis of test data collected during developmental testing of structural improvements for the RMMV and the RMMV recovery system as well as MVCS upgrades is still in progress. The Navy expects to issue a formal test report in 2QFY14.

• Even if this MCM package meets all of its final increment requirements, legacy systems will be needed to perform the full range of mine clearance operations.[80]

Defense-Acquisition Policy Lessons of LCS Program

Another issue for Congress concerns what defense-acquisition policy lessons, if any, the LCS program may offer to policy makers, particularly in terms of the rapid acquisition strategy that the Navy pursued for the LCS program, which aimed at reducing acquisition cycle time (i.e., the amount of time between starting the program and getting the first ship into service).

One possible perspective is that the LCS program demonstrated that reducing acquisition cycle time can be done. Supporters of this perspective might argue that under a traditional Navy ship acquisition approach, the Navy might have spent five or six years developing a design for a new frigate or corvette, and perhaps another five years building the lead ship, for a total acquisition cycle time of perhaps 10 to 11 years. For a program announced in November 2001, this would have resulted in the first ship entering service in between late 2011 and late 2012. In contrast, supporters of this perspective might argue, LCS-1 entered service on November 8, 2008, about seven years after the program was announced, and LCS-2 entered service on January 16, 2010, a little more than eight years after the program announced. Supporters of this perspective might argue that this reduction in acquisition cycle time was accomplished even though the LCS incorporates major innovations compared to previous larger Navy surface combatants in terms of reduced crew size, "plug-and-fight" mission package modularity, high-speed propulsion, and (in the case of LCS-2) hull form and hull materials.

Another possible perspective is that the LCS program demonstrated the risks or consequences of attempting to reduce acquisition cycle time. Supporters of this perspective might argue that the program's rapid acquisition strategy resulted in design-construction concurrency (i.e., building the lead ships before their designs were fully developed), a practice long known to increase risks in defense acquisition programs. Supporters of this perspective might argue that the cost growth, design issues, and construction-quality issues experienced by the first LCSs were due in substantial part to design-construction concurrency, and that these problems embarrassed the Navy and reduced the Navy's credibility in defending other acquisition programs. They might argue that the challenges the Navy faces today in terms of developing an LCS concept of operations (CONOPS),[81] LCS manning and training policies, and LCS maintenance and logistics plans were increased by the rapid acquisition strategy, because these matters were partly deferred

---

[80] Department of Defense, Director, Operational Test & Evaluation, □□ □□□*Annal Report*, January 2014, pp. 199-200.

[81] A CONOPS is a detailed understanding of how to use the ship to accomplish various missions.

to later years (i.e., to today) while the Navy moved to put LCSs into production. Supporters of this perspective might argue that the costs of the rapid acquisition strategy are not offset by very much in terms of a true reduction in acquisition cycle time, because the first LCS to be equipped with a mission package that has reached IOC (initial operational capability) will not occur until late FY2014—almost 13 years after the LCS program was announced. Supporters of this perspective could argue that the Navy could have avoided many of the program's early problems and current challenges—and could have had a fully equipped first ship enter service in 2011 or 2012—if it had instead pursued a traditional acquisition approach for a new frigate or corvette. They could argue that the LCS program validated, for defense acquisition, the guideline from the world of business management that if an effort aims at obtaining something fast, cheap, and good, it will succeed in getting no more than two of these things,[82] or, more simply, that the LCS program validated the general saying that haste makes waste.

A third possible perspective is that the LCS program offers few if any defense-acquisition policy lessons because the LCS differs so much from other Navy ships and the Navy (and DOD generally) consequently is unlikely to attempt a program like the LCS in the future. Supporters of this perspective might argue that the risks of design-construction concurrency have long been known, and that the experience of the LCS program did not provide a new lesson in this regard so much as a reminder of an old one. They might argue that the cost growth and construction delays experienced by LCS-1 were caused not simply by the program's rapid acquisition strategy, but by a variety of factors (see "Reasons for Cost Growth" in **Appendix A**), including an incorrectly made reduction gear[83] from a supplier firm that forced the shipbuilder to build the lead ship in a significantly revised and sub-optimal construction sequence.

Legislative Activity for FY2015

FY2015 Budget Request

The Navy's proposed FY2015 budget requests $1,421.7 million in procurement funding for the procurement of three LCSs in FY2015, or an average of $475.7 million per ship, in the Shipbuilding and Conversion, Navy (SCN) appropriation account. The budget requests an additional $93.0 million in the SCN account to complete the costs of LCSs funded in prior years; this request forms part of a larger Navy request for $1,007.3 million in cost-to-complete funding for various Navy shipbuilding programs.

The Navy's proposed FY2015 budget also requests a total of $99.6 million in procurement funding for LCS mission modules in lines 34 through 37 of the Other Procurement, Navy (OPN) appropriation account.

---

[82] The guideline is sometimes referred to in the business world as "Fast, cheap, good—pick two."

[83] A ship's reduction gear is a large, heavy gear that reduces the high-speed revolutions of the ship's turbine engines to the lower-speed revolutions of its propulsors.

FY2015 National Defense Authorization Act (H.R. 4435/S. 2410)

House

The House Armed Services Committee, in its report (H.Rept. 113-446 of May 13, 2014) on H.R. 4435, recommends $977.0 million in procurement funding for the procurement of two LCSs in FY2015—a reduction of one LCS and $450 million from the Navy's request. (Page 395, line 009.) The report recommends an additional $100 million in advance procurement (AP) funding for the procurement of an LCS in a future fiscal year. (Page 395, line 009A.) The report also recommends approving the Navy's request for $93.0 million in procurement funding to complete the costs of LCSs funded in prior years. (Page 426, line 021.) The report recommends approving the Navy's request for procurement funding for LCS mission modules in the OPN account. (Page 397, lines 34 through 37.)

Section 125 of H.R. 4435 as reported states:

> SEC. 125. LIMITATION ON AVAILABILITY OF FUNDS FOR MISSION MODULES FOR LITTORAL COMBAT SHIP.
>
> None of the funds authorized to be appropriated by this Act or otherwise made available for fiscal year 2015 for the procurement of additional mission modules for the Littoral Combat Ship program may be obligated or expended until the Secretary of the Navy submits to the congressional defense committees each of the following:
>
> (1) The Milestone B program goals for cost, schedule, and performance for each increment.
>
> (2) Certification by the Director of Operational Test and Evaluation with respect to the total number for each module type that is required to perform all necessary operational testing.

Section 126 of H.R. 4435 as reported states

> SEC. 126. EXTENSION OF LIMITATION ON AVAILABILITY OF FUNDS FOR LITTORAL COMBAT SHIP.
>
> Section 124(a) of the National Defense Authorization Act for Fiscal Year 2014 (P.L. 113-66; 127 Stat. 693) is amended by striking `this Act or otherwise made available for fiscal year 2014' and inserting `this Act, the Howard P. `Buck' McKeon National Defense Authorization Act for Fiscal Year 2015, or otherwise made available for fiscal years 2014 or 2015'-

H.Rept. 113-446 states:

> *⬚ittoral ⬚om⬚at ⬚ip*
>
> The committee is concerned about the survivability, lethality and endurance of the Navy's Littoral Combat Ship (LCS), as noted by the Government Accountability Office and others. In February 2014, after reviewing preliminary assessments and evaluations of the LCS, the Secretary of Defense reduced the total number of LCS seaframes to 32 from the planned procurement of 52 and also directed the Navy to submit alternate proposals to procure "a capable and lethal small surface combatant generally consistent with the capabilities of a frigate." The Secretary noted the importance of not only presence but capability and power projection as the foundation of the Navy's effectiveness and directed the Navy to study

options to include a completely new design, existing ship designs (including the LCS), and a modified LCS. The Chief of Naval Operations has directed a Small Surface Combatant Task Force to report on these results by July 31, 2014.

Therefore, the committee directs the Comptroller General of the United States to provide a report to the congressional defense committees by April 1, 2015, that examines the Department of the Navy's study and its implications for the procurement of future small surface combatants. This report should assess:

(1) The study's methodologies and key assumptions;

(2) Any alternate ship design(s) and modifications to the Littoral Combat Ship that the Navy evaluated, including expectations of cost, schedule, and requirements; and

(3) The extent to which the study was consistent with the approach of a formal analysis of alternatives, as set forth in the Department of Defense acquisition policy. (Pages 29-30)

Senate

The Senate Armed Services Committee, in its report (S.Rept. 113-176 of June 2, 2014) on S. 2410, recommends approving the Navy's request for FY2015 procurement funding for the procurement of three LCSs. (Page 323, line 9.) The report recommends approving the Navy's request for $93.0 million in procurement funding to complete the costs of LCSs funded in prior years. (Page 324, line 021.) The report recommends approving the Navy's request for procurement funding for LCS mission modules in the OPN account. (Pages 325-326, lines 34 through 37.)

Section 122 of S. 2410 as reported states:

> SEC. 122. REPORT ON TEST EVALUATION MASTER PLAN FOR LITTORAL COMBAT SHIP SEAFRAMES AND MISSION MODULES.
>
> (a) In General- Not later than 60 days after the date of the enactment of this Act, the Director of Operational Test and Evaluation shall submit to the congressional defense committees a report on the test evaluation master plan for the seaframes and mission modules for the Littoral Combat Ship program.
>
> (b) Elements- The report required under subsection (a) shall include the following elements:
>
> (1) A description of the Navy's progress with respect to the test evaluation master plan.
>
> (2) An assessment of whether or not completion of the test evaluation master plan will demonstrate operational effectiveness and operational suitability for both seaframes and each mission module.

Section 1023 of S. 2410 as reported states:

> SEC. 1023. OPERATIONAL READINESS OF LITTORAL COMBAT SHIPS ON EXTENDED DEPLOYMENTS.
>
> (a) Authority- Subsection (a) of section 7310 of title 10, United States Code, is amended--

(1) in the subsection heading, by inserting `Under the Jurisdiction of the Secretary of the Navy' after `Vessels';

(2) by striking `A naval vessel' and inserting `(1) Except as provided in paragraph (2), a naval vessel'; and

(3) by adding at the end the following new paragraph:

`(2)(A) Subject to subparagraph (B), in the case of a naval vessel that is classified as a Littoral Combat Ship and is operating on deployment, corrective and preventive maintenance or repair (whether intermediate or depot level) and facilities maintenance may be performed on the vessel--

`(i) in a foreign shipyard;

`(ii) at a facility outside of a foreign shipyard; or

`(iii) at any other facility convenient to the vessel.

`(B)(i) Corrective and preventive maintenance or repair may be performed on a vessel as described in subparagraph (A) only if the work is performed by United States Government personnel or United States contractor personnel.

`(ii) Facilities maintenance may be performed by a foreign contractor on a vessel as described in subparagraph (A) only as approved by the Secretary of the Navy.'.

(b) Definitions- Such section is further amended by adding at the end the following new subsection:

`(d) Definitions- In this section:

`(1) The term `corrective and preventive maintenance or repair' means--

`(A) maintenance or repair actions performed as a result of a failure in order to return or restore equipment to acceptable performance levels; and

`(B) scheduled maintenance or repair actions intended to prevent or discover functional failures, including scheduled periodic maintenance requirements and integrated class maintenance plan tasks that are time-directed maintenance actions.

`(2) The term `facilities maintenance' means--

`(A) preservation or corrosion control efforts, encompassing surface preparation and preservation of the structural facility to minimize effects of corrosion; and

`(B) cleaning services, encompassing--

`(i) light surface cleaning of ship structures and compartments; and

`(ii) deep cleaning of bilges to remove dirt, oily waste, and other foreign matter.'.

(c) Clerical Amendments-

(1) SECTION HEADING- The heading of such section is amended to read as follows:

`Sec. 7310. Overhaul, repair, and maintenance of vessels in foreign shipyards and facilities: restrictions; exceptions'.

(2) TABLE OF SECTIONS- The table of sections at the beginning of chapter 633 of such title is amended by striking the item relating to section 7310 and inserting the following:

`7310. Overhaul, repair, and maintenance of vessels in foreign shipyards and facilities: restrictions; exceptions.'.

Regarding Section 1023, S.Rept. 113-176 states:

Operational readiness of Littoral Combat Ships on extended deployments (sec. 1023)

The committee recommends a provision that would provide additional flexibility for the Secretary of the Navy to maintain Littoral Combat Ships (LCS) by allowing government personnel or U.S. contractor personnel to conduct corrective and preventive maintenance on an LCS vessel regardless of the ship's location.

Because an LCS vessel has a smaller crew than other Navy vessels, much of the corrective and preventative maintenance must be performed by personnel not in the ship's force. The Secretary of Navy needs added flexibility in conducting this maintenance to ensure that the Navy can sustain readiness, particularly on forward-deployed LCS vessels. (Page 166)

Appendix A. Cost Growth on LCS Sea Frames in FY2007-FY2013 Budgets

This appendix presents details on cost growth on the first few LCS sea frames in the FY2007-FY2012 budget submissions.

FY2007 Budget

The proposed FY2007 Navy budget, submitted in February 2006, showed that:

- the estimate for the first LCS had increased from $215.5 million in the FY2005 budget and $212.5 million in the FY2006 budget to $274.5 million in the FY2007 budget—an increase of about 27% from the FY2005 figure and about 29% form the FY2006 figure;

- the estimate for the second LCS increased from $213.7 million in the FY2005 budget and $256.5 million in the FY2006 budget to $278.1 million—an increase of about 30% from the FY2005 figure and about 8% from the FY2006 figure; and

- the estimate for follow-on ships scheduled for FY2009-FY2011, when the LCS program was to have reached a planned maximum annual procurement rate of six ships per year, had increased from $223.3 million in the FY2006 budget to $298 million—an increase of about 33%.

The Navy stated in early 2006 that the cost increase from the FY2006 budget to the FY2007 budget was due mostly to the fact that LCS procurement costs in the FY2006 budget did not include items that are traditionally included in the so-called end cost—the total budgeted procurement cost—of a Navy shipbuilding program, such as Navy program-management costs, an allowance for changes, and escalation (inflation). The absence of these costs from the FY2006 LCS budget submission raised certain potential oversight issues for Congress.[84]

---

[84] These oversight issues included the following:

—Why were these costs excluded? Was this a budget-preparation oversight? If so, how could such an oversight occur, given the many people involved in Navy budget preparation and review, and why did it occur on the LCS program but not other programs? Was anyone held accountable for this oversight, and if so, how? If this was not an oversight, then what was the reason?

—Did the Navy believe there was no substantial risk of penalty for submitting to Congress a budget presentation for a shipbuilding program that, for whatever reason, significantly underestimated procurement costs?

—Do LCS procurement costs in the budget now include all costs that, under traditional budgeting practices, should be included? If not, what other costs are still unacknowledged?

—Have personnel or other resources from other Navy programs been used for the LCS program in any way? If so, have the costs of these personnel or other resources been fully charged to the LCS program and fully reflected in LCS program costs shown in the budget?

FY2008 Budget

On January 11, 2007, the Navy reported that LCS-1 was experiencing "considerable cost overruns." The Navy subsequently stated that the estimated shipyard construction cost of LCS-1 had grown to $350 million to $375 million. This suggested that the end cost of LCS-1—which also includes costs for things such as Navy program-management costs and an allowance for changes—could be in excess of $400 million. The Navy did not publicly provide a precise cost overrun figure for LCS 2, but it stated that the cost overrun on LCSs 1 and 2 was somewhere between 50% and 75%, depending on the baseline that is used to measure the overrun.

GAO testified in July 2007 that according to its own analysis of Navy data, the combined cost of LCSs 1 and 2 had increased from $472 million to $1,075 million—an increase of 128%.[85] CBO testified in July 2007 that:

> Several months ago, press reports indicated that the cost could well exceed $400 million each for the first two LCS sea frames. Recently, the Navy requested that the cost cap for the fifth and sixth sea frames be raised to $460 million, which suggests that the Navy's estimate of the acquisition cost for the first two LCSs would be around $600 million apiece....
>
> As of this writing, the Navy has not publicly released an estimate for the LCS program that incorporates the most recent cost growth, other than its request to raise the cost caps for the fifth and sixth ships. CBO estimates that with that growth included, the first two LCSs would cost about $630 million each, excluding mission modules but including outfitting, postdelivery, and various nonrecurring costs associated with the first ships of the class. As the program advances, with a settled design and higher annual rates of production, the average cost per ship is likely to decline. Excluding mission modules, the 55 LCSs in the Navy's plan would cost an average of $450 million each, CBO estimates.[86]

FY2009 Budget

The proposed FY2009 budget, submitted in February 2008, showed that the estimated end costs of LCS-1 and LCS-2 had increased to $531 million and $507 million, respectively—or to $631 million and $636 million, respectively, when OF/PD (outfitting and post-delivery) and FSD MSSIT (Final System Design Mission Systems and Ship Integration Team) costs are included, or to $606 million and $582 million, respectively, when OF/PD costs are included, but FSD MSSIT costs are not included.

FY2010 Budget

The proposed FY2010 budget, submitted in May 2009, showed that the estimated end costs of LCS-1 and LCS-2 had increased to $537 million and $575 million, respectively (or to $637

---

[85] Defense Acquisitions[:] Realistic Business Cases Needed to Execute Navy Shipbuilding Programs, Statement of Paul L. Francis, Director, Acquisition and Sourcing Management Team, Testimony Before the Subcommittee on Seapower and Expeditionary Forces, Committee on Armed Services, House of Representatives, July 24, 2007 (GAO-07-943T), pp. 4 and 22.

[86] Statement of J. Michael Gilmore, Assistant Director for National Security, and Eric J. Labs, Senior Analyst, [on] The Navy's 2008 Shipbuilding Plan and Key Ship Programs, before the Subcommittee on Seapower and Expeditionary Forces Committee on Armed Services U.S. House of Representatives, July 24, 2007, p. 18.

million and $704 million, respectively, when OF/PD and FSD MSSIT costs are included, or to $612 million and $650 million, respectively, when OF/PD costs are included, but FSD MSSIT costs are not included). CBO reported on June 9, 2008, that:

> Historical experience indicates that cost growth in the LCS program is likely. In particular, using the lead ship of the FFG-7 Oliver Hazard Perry class frigate as an analogy, historical cost-to-weight relationships indicate that the Navy's original cost target for the LCS of $260 million in 2009 dollars (or $220 million in 2005 dollars) was optimistic. The first FFG-7 cost about $670 million in 2009 dollars to build, or about $250 million per thousand tons, including combat systems. Applying that metric to the LCS program suggests that the lead ships would cost about $600 million apiece, including the cost of one mission module. Thus, in this case, the use of a historical cost-to-weight relationship produces an estimate that is less than the actual costs of the first LCSs to date but substantially more than the Navy's original estimate.
>
> Based on actual costs the Navy has incurred for the LCS program, CBO estimates that the first two LCSs could cost about $700 million each, including outfitting and postdelivery and various nonrecurring costs associated with first ships of a class but excluding mission modules. However, as of May 1, 2008, LCS-1 was 83 percent complete and LCS-2 was 68 percent complete. Thus, additional cost growth is possible, and CBO's estimate reflects that cost risk.
>
> Overall, CBO estimates that the LCSs in the Navy's plan would cost about $550 million each, on average, excluding mission modules. That estimate assumes that the Navy would select one of the two existing designs and make no changes. As the program advanced with a settled design and higher annual rates of production, average ship costs would probably decline. If the Navy decided to make changes to that design, however, the costs of building future ships could be higher than CBO now estimates.[87]

FY2011 Budget

The proposed FY2011 budget, submitted in February 2010, showed that the estimated end cost of LCS-1 remained unchanged from the previous year at $537 million, and that the estimated end cost of LCS-2 had increased to $607 million. These two figures become $656 million and $736 million, respectively, when OF/PD and FSD MSSIT costs are included, or $631 million and $682 million, respectively, when OF/PD costs are included, but FSD MSSIT costs are not included. The Navy's FY2011 budget submission states that OF/PD and FSD MSSIT costs are non-end cost items, and that FSD MSSIT costs for LCS-1 and LCS-2 "are not true construction costs and are [instead] costs associated with design completion."[88]

FY2012 Budget

The proposed FY2012 budget, submitted in February 2011, showed that the estimated end cost of LCS-1 remained unchanged from the previous year at $537 million, and that the estimated end

---

[87] Congressional Budget Office, *Reso⬜rce ⬜mplications of t⬜e Na⬜y's ⬜iscal ⬜ear ⬜⬜⬜ ⬜ip⬜il⬜in⬜ ⬜lan*, June 8, 2008, pp. 26-27.

[88] Source: Department of Navy, *Department of t⬜e Na⬜y ⬜iscal ⬜ear ⬜⬜⬜⬜⬜⬜ ⬜⬜⬜et ⬜stimates⬜⬜e⬜r⬜ary ⬜⬜⬜⬜ ⬜stification of ⬜stimates⬜Researc⬜De⬜elopment⬜⬜est & ⬜⬜al⬜ation⬜Na⬜y⬜⬜⬜⬜et Acti⬜ity ⬜*, Exhibit R-2A, RDT&E Project Justification, PE 0603581N: Littoral Combat Ship (LCS), pages 34-35 of 46 (PDF pages 552-553 of 1054).

cost of LCS-2 had increased to $653 million. These two figures become $670.4 million and $808.8 million, respectively, when OF/PD and FSD MSSIT costs are included, or $645.4 million and $754.8 million, respectively, when OF/PD costs are included, but FSD MSSIT costs are not included. The Navy's FY2011 budget submission states that OF/PD and FSD MSSIT costs are non-end cost items, and that FSD MSSIT costs for LCS-1 and LCS-2 "are not true construction costs and are [instead] costs associated with design completion."[89]

FY2013 Budget

The proposed FY2013 budget, submitted in February 2012, showed that the estimated end costs of LCS-1 and LCS -2 remained unchanged from the previous year at $537 million and $653 million, respectively. These two figures become $670.4 million and $813.4 million, respectively, when OF/PD and FSD MSSIT costs are included, or $645.4 million and $759.4 million, respectively, when OF/PD costs are included, but FSD MSSIT costs are not included. The Navy's FY2012 budget submission states that OF/PD and FSD MSSIT costs are non-end cost items, and that FSD MSSIT costs for LCS-1 and LCS-2 "are not true construction costs and are [instead] costs associated with design completion."[90]

Reasons for Cost Growth

Various reasons have been cited for cost growth in the LCS program, including the following:

- **Unrealistically low original estimate.** Some observers believe that the original cost estimate of $220 million for the LCS sea frame was unrealistically low. If so, a potential follow-on question would be whether the LCS represents a case of "low-balling"—using an unrealistically low cost estimate in the early stages of a proposed weapon program to help the program win approval and become an established procurement effort.

- **Impact of Naval Vessel Rules (NVR).** Navy and industry officials have attributed some of the cost growth to the impact of applying new Naval Vessel Rules (NVR)—essentially, new rules specifying the construction standards for the ship—to the LCS program. The NVR issued for the LCS program incorporated, among other things, an increase in the survivability standard (the ability to withstand damage) to which LCSs were to be built. Building the ship to a higher survivability standard represented a change in requirements for the ship that led to many design changes, including changes that made ship more rugged and more complex in terms of its damage-control systems. In addition, Navy and industry officials have testified, the timing of the issuing of NVR created a situation of concurrency between design and construction in the LCS program, meaning that the ship was being designed at the same time that the shipyard was

---

[89] Source: Department of Defense, *Department of Defense □iscal □ear □□□□□□□□□□□et □stimates□e□r□ary □□□□ Na□y □stification □oo□□ol□me □Researc□De□elopment□est & □□al□ation□Na□y□□□□et Acti□ity □,* Exhibit R-2A, RDT&E Project Justification, PE 0603581N: Littoral Combat Ship (LCS), page 33 of 42 (PDF page 469 of 888).

[90] Source: Department of Defense, *Department of Defense □iscal □ear □□□□□□□□□resi□ent□s □□□□et □□mission□ □e□r□ary □□□□Na□y □stification □oo□□ol□me □Researc□De□elopment□est & □□al□ation□Na□y□□□□et Acti□ity □,* Exhibit R-2A, RDT&E Project Justification, PE 0603581N: Littoral Combat Ship (LCS), pages 39 and 40 of 48 (PDF pages 491 and 492 of 940).

---

attempting to build it—a situation long known to be a potential cause of cost growth. This concurrency, Navy officials testified, was a consequence of the compressed construction schedule for the LCS program, which in turn reflected an urgency about getting LCSs into the fleet to meet critical mission demands.

- **Improperly manufactured reduction gear.** Navy and industry officials testified that cost growth on LCS-1 was partly due to a main reduction gear[91] that was incorrectly manufactured and had to be replaced, forcing a reordering of the construction sequence for the various major sections of the ship.

- **Increased costs for materials.** Some observers have attributed part of the cost growth in the program to higher-than-estimated costs for steel and other materials that are used in building the ships.

- **Emphasis on meeting schedule combined with cost-plus contract.** Some portion of cost growth on LCS-1 has been attributed to a combination of a Navy emphasis on meeting the ship's aggressive construction schedule and the Navy's use of a cost-plus contract to build the ship.[92]

- **Shipyard Performance.** Shipyard performance and supervision of the LCS shipyards by the LCS team leaders and the Navy has been cited as another cause of cost growth.[93]

July 2007 GAO Testimony

GAO testified in July 2007 that:

> We have frequently reported on the wisdom of using a solid, executable business case before committing resources to a new product development effort....
>
> A sound business case would establish and resource a knowledge-based approach at the outset of a program. We would define such a business case as firm requirements, mature technologies, and an acquisition strategy that provides sufficient time and money for design activities before construction start. The business case is the essential first step in any

---

[91] A ship's reduction gear is a large, heavy gear that reduces the high-speed revolutions of the ship's turbine engines to the lower-speed revolutions of its propulsors.

[92] The Senate Armed Services Committee, as part of its discussion of the LCS program in its report (S.Rept. 110-77 of June 5, 2007) on the FY2008 defense authorization bill (S. 1547), stated:

> Reviewing this LCS situation will undoubtedly result in a new set of "lessons learned"· that the acquisition community will dutifully try to implement. However, the committee has previously expressed concerns about the LCS concept and the LCS acquisition strategy. The LCS situation may be more a case of "lessons lost." Long ago, we knew that we should not rush to sign a construction contract before we have solidified requirements. We also knew that the contractors will respond to incentives, and that if the incentives are focused on maintaining schedules and not on controlling cost, cost growth on a cost-plus contract should surprise no one. After the fact, everyone appears ready to agree that the original ship construction schedule for the lead ship was overly aggressive. (Page 98)

[93] See Katherine McIntire Peters, "Navy's Top Officer Sees Lessons In Shipbuilding Program Failures," ☐o☐ernment☐ec☐ti☐e.com, September 24, 2008; Christopher J. Castelli, "Audit Exposes Failed Management of Troubled Littoral Warship," ☐nsi☐e t☐e Na☐y, February 4, 2008; Christopher J. Castelli, "Audit Reveals Both LCS and Industry Teams Violated Management Rules," ☐nsi☐e t☐e ☐enta☐on, July 10, 2008 (reprinted in essentially identical form, with the same headline, in the July 14, 2008, issue of sister publication ☐nsi☐e t☐e Na☐y).

---

acquisition program that sets the stage for the remaining stages of a program, namely the business or contracting arrangements and actual execution or performance. If the business case is not sound, the contract will not correct the problem and execution will be subpar. This does not mean that all potential problems can be eliminated and perfection achieved, but rather that sound business cases can get the Navy better shipbuilding outcomes and better return on investment. If any one element of the business case is weak, problems can be expected in construction. The need to meet schedule is one of the main reasons why programs cannot execute their business cases. This pattern was clearly evident in both the LPD 17 [amphibious ship] and LCS programs. In both cases, the program pushed ahead with production even when design problems arose or key equipment was not available when needed. Short cuts, such as doing technology development concurrently with design and construction, are taken to meet schedule. In the end, problems occur that cannot be resolved within compressed, optimistic schedules. Ultimately, when a schedule is set that cannot accommodate program scope, delivering an initial capability is delayed and higher costs are incurred....

What happens when the elements of a solid business case are not present? Unfortunately, the results have been all too visible in the LPD 17 and the LCS. Ship construction in these programs has been hampered throughout by design instability and program management challenges that can be traced back to flawed business cases. The Navy moved forward with ambitious schedules for constructing LPD 17 and LCS despite significant challenges in stabilizing the designs for these ships. As a result, construction work has been performed out of sequence and significant rework has been required, disrupting the optimal construction sequence and application of lessons learned for follow-on vessels in these programs....

In the LCS program, design instability resulted from a flawed business case as well as changes to Navy requirements. From the outset, the Navy sought to concurrently design and construct two lead ships in the LCS program in an effort to rapidly meet pressing needs in the mine countermeasures, antisubmarine warfare, and surface warfare mission areas. The Navy believed it could manage this approach, even with little margin for error, because it considered each LCS to be an adaptation of an existing high-speed ferry design. It has since been realized that transforming a high-speed ferry into a capable, networked, survivable warship was quite a complex venture. Implementation of new Naval Vessel Rules (design guidelines) further complicated the Navy's concurrent design-build strategy for LCS. These rules required program officials to redesign major elements of each LCS design to meet enhanced survivability requirements, even after construction had begun on the first ship. While these requirements changes improved the robustness of LCS designs, they contributed to out of sequence work and rework on the lead ships. The Navy failed to fully account for these changes when establishing its $220 million cost target and 2-year construction cycle for the lead ships.

Complicating LCS construction was a compressed and aggressive schedule. When design standards were clarified with the issuance of Naval Vessel Rules and major equipment deliveries were delayed (e.g., main reduction gears), adjustments to the schedule were not made. Instead, with the first LCS, the Navy and shipbuilder continued to focus on achieving the planned schedule, accepting the higher costs associated with out of sequence work and rework. This approach enabled the Navy to achieve its planned launch date for the first Littoral Combat Ship, but required it to sacrifice its desired level of outfitting. Program officials report that schedule pressures also drove low outfitting levels on the second Littoral Combat Ship design as well, although rework requirements have been less intensive to date. However, because remaining work on the first two ships will now have to be completed out-of-sequence, the initial schedule gains most likely will be offset by increased labor hours to finish these ships.

The difficulties and costs discussed above relate to the LCS seaframe only. This program is unique in that the ship's mission equipment is being developed and funded separately from the seaframe. The Navy faces additional challenges integrating mission packages with the ships, which could further increase costs and delay delivery of new antisubmarine warfare, mine countermeasures, and surface warfare capabilities to the fleet. These mission packages are required to meet a weight requirement of 180 metric tons or less and require 35 personnel or less to operate them. However, the Navy estimates that the mine countermeasures mission package may require an additional 13 metric tons of weight and seven more operator personnel in order to deploy the full level of promised capability. Because neither of the competing ship designs can accommodate these increases, the Navy may be forced to reevaluate its planned capabilities for LCS.[94]

---

[94] Defense Acquisitions[:] Realistic Business Cases Needed to Execute Navy Shipbuilding Programs, Statement of Paul L. Francis, Director, Acquisition and Sourcing Management Team, Testimony Before the Subcommittee on Seapower and Expeditionary Forces, Committee on Armed Services, House of Representatives, July 24, 2007 (GAO-07-943T), pp. 8-11.

Appendix B. 2007 Program Restructuring and Ship Cancellations

The Navy substantially restructured the LCS program in 2007 in response to significant cost growth and delays in constructing the first LCS sea frames. This restructuring led to the cancellation of four LCSs that were funded in FY2006 and FY2007. A fifth LCS, funded in FY2008, was cancelled in 2008. This appendix presents the details of the program restructuring and ship cancellations.

2007 Program Restructuring

March 2007 Navy Restructuring Plan

In response to significant cost growth and schedule delays in the building of the first LCSs that first came to light in January 2007 (see next section), the Navy in March 2007 announced a plan for restructuring the LCS program that:

- canceled the two LCSs funded in FY2007 and redirected the funding for those two ships to pay for cost overruns on earlier LCSs;

- announced an intention to lift a 90-day stop-work order that the Navy had placed on LCS-3 in January 2007—provided that the Navy reached an agreement with the Lockheed-led industry team by April 12, 2007, to restructure the contract for building LCSs 1 and 3 from a cost-plus type contract into a fixed price incentive (FPI)-type contract—or terminate construction of LCS-3 if an agreement on a restructured contract could not be reached with the Lockheed team by April 12, 2007;

- announced an intention to seek to restructure the contract with the General Dynamics-led industry team for building LCSs 2 and 4 into an FPI-type contract—if LCSs 2 and 4 experienced cost growth comparable to that of LCSs 1 and 3—and, if such a restructuring were sought, terminate construction of LCS-4 if an agreement on a restructured contract for LCS-2 and LCS-4 could not be reached;

- reduced the number of LCSs requested for FY2008 from three to two (for the same requested FY2008 procurement funding of $910.5 million), and the number to be requested for FY2009 from six to three; and

- announced an intention to conduct an operational evaluation to select a favored design for the LCS that would be procured in FY2010 and subsequent years, and to conduct a full and open follow-on competition among bidders for the right to build that design.[95]

---

[95] Source: Navy briefing to CRS and Congressional Budget Office (CBO) on Navy's proposed LCS program restructuring plan, March 21, 2007.

April 2007 Termination of LCS-3

On April 12, 2007, the Navy announced that it had not reached an agreement with Lockheed on a restructured FPI-type contract for LCS-1 and LCS-3, and consequently was terminating construction of LCS-3.[96] (The Navy subsequently began referring to the ship as having been partially terminated—a reference to the fact that Lockheed was allowed to continue procuring certain components for LCS-3, so that a complete set of these components would be on hand to be incorporated into the next LCS built to the Lockheed design.) (The designation LCS-3 is now being reused to refer to one of the two LCSs procured in FY2009.)

November 2007 Termination of LCS-4

In late September 2007, it was reported that the Navy on September 19 had sent a letter to General Dynamics to initiate negotiations on restructuring the contract for building LCSs 2 and 4 into an FPI-type contract. The negotiations reportedly were to be completed by October 19, 2007—30 days from September 19.[97] On November 1, 2007, the Navy announced that it had not reached an agreement with General Dynamics on a restructured FPI-type contract for LCS-2 and LCS-4, and consequently was terminating construction of LCS-4.[98] (The designation LCS-4 is now being reused to refer to one of the two LCSs procured in FY2009.)

Cancellation of Prior-Year Ships

Table B-1 below summarizes the status of the nine LCSs funded by Congress from FY2005 through FY2009. As shown in the table, of the nine ships, five were later canceled, leaving four ships in place through FY2009—LCSs 1 and 2, and the two LCSs funded in FY2009. Ship designations LCS-3 and LCS-4 are being reused as the designations for the two ships funded in FY2009.

---

[96] Department of Defense News Release No. 422-07, April 12, 2007, "Navy Terminates Littoral Combat Ship 3."

[97] Geoff Fein, "Navy Seeking To Negotiate FPI Contract With General Dynamics," *Defense Daily*, September 24, 2007; Geoff Fein, "Navy, General Dynamics Meet To Discuss New LCS Fixed Price Structure," *Defense Daily*, September 27, 2007; Tony Capaccio, "General Dynamics Urged To Take Fixed Price On Warship Contract," □loom□er□News, September 28, 2007; Jason Sherman, "Navy, General Dynamics Discuss Fixed-Price Contract For LCS," □nsi□e t□e Na□y, October 1, 2007.

[98] Department of Defense News Release No. 1269-07, November 1, 2007, "Navy Terminates Littoral Combat Ship (LCS 4) Contract."

Table B-1. Status of LCSs Funded in FY2005-FY2009

FY funded	Navy hull designation	Status
2005	LCS-1	**Commissioned into service** on November 8, 2008.
2006	LCS-2	**Commissioned into service** on January 16, 2010.
	LCS-3 (not the same ship as LCS-3 below)	**Canceled by Navy** in April 2007 after being placed under contract due to inability to come to agreement with contractor on revised (fixed-price) contract terms for LCSs 1 and 3.
	LCS-4 (not the same ship as LCS-4 below)	**Canceled by Navy** in November 2007 after being placed under contract due to inability to come to agreement with contractor on revised (fixed-price) contract terms for LCSs 2 and 4.
2007	none (ship canceled before being placed under contract)	**Canceled by Navy** in March 2007 before being placed under contract as part of Navy's LCS program restructuring; funds reapplied to cover other program costs.
	none (ship canceled before being placed under contract)	**Canceled by Navy** in March 2007 before being placed under contract as part of Navy's LCS program restructuring; funds reapplied to cover other program costs.
2008	LCS-5 (for a while, at least, although the ship was canceled before being placed under contract; the ship designation is now being used for the first of the two ships funded in FY2010)	**Canceled by Navy following Congress's decision** in September 2008, as part of its action on the FY2009 defense appropriations bill, to rescind the funding for the ship.
2009	LCS-3 (not the same ship as LCS-3 above; the ship designation is being reused)	**Commissioned into service** on August 6, 2012.
	LCS-4 (not the same ship as LCS-4 above; the ship designation is being reused)	**Under construction.**

Source: Prepared by CRS.

Appendix C. Down Select Acquisition Strategy Announced in September 2009

This appendix presents additional background information on the down select acquisition strategy announced by the Navy on September 16, 2009.

DOD and Navy Background Information

A September 16, 2009, DOD news release on the proposed down select strategy stated:

> The Navy announced today it will down select between the two Littoral Combat Ship (LCS) designs in fiscal 2010. The current LCS seaframe construction solicitation [for the FY2010 LCSs] will be cancelled and a new solicitation will be issued. At down select, a single prime contractor and shipyard will be awarded a fixed price incentive contract for up to 10 ships with two ships in fiscal 2010 and options through fiscal 2014. This decision was reached after careful review of the fiscal 2010 industry bids, consideration of total program costs, and ongoing discussions with Congress.
>
> "This change to increase competition is required so we can build the LCS at an affordable price," said Ray Mabus, secretary of the Navy. "LCS is vital to our Navy's future. It must succeed."
>
> "Both ships meet our operational requirements and we need LCS now to meet the warfighters' needs," said Adm. Gary Roughead, chief of naval operations. "Down selecting now will improve affordability and will allow us to build LCS at a realistic cost and not compromise critical warfighting capabilities."
>
> The Navy cancelled the solicitation to procure up to three LCS Flight 0+ ships in fiscal 2010 due to affordability. Based on proposals received this summer, it was not possible to execute the LCS program under the current acquisition strategy and given the expectation of constrained budgets. The new LCS acquisition strategy improves affordability by competitively awarding a larger number of ships across several years to one source. The Navy will accomplish this goal by issuing a new fixed price incentive solicitation for a down select to one of the two designs beginning in fiscal 2010.
>
> Both industry teams will have the opportunity to submit proposals for the fiscal 2010 ships under the new solicitation. The selected industry team will deliver a quality technical data package, allowing the Navy to open competition for a second source for the selected design beginning in fiscal 2012. The winner of the down select will be awarded a contract for up to 10 ships from fiscal 2010 through fiscal 2014, and also provide combat systems for up to five additional ships provided by a second source. Delivery of LCS 2, along with construction of LCS 3 and LCS 4 will not be affected by the decision. This plan ensures the best value for the Navy, continues to fill critical warfighting gaps, reduces program ownership costs, and meets the spirit and intent of the Weapons System Acquisition Reform Act of 2009....
>
> The Navy remains committed to the LCS program and the requirement for 55 of these ships to provide combatant commanders with the capability to defeat anti-access threats in the littorals, including fast surface craft, quiet submarines and various types of mines. The

Navy's acquisition strategy will be guided by cost and performance of the respective designs as well as options for sustaining competition throughout the life of the program.[99]

A September 16, 2009, email from the Navy to CRS provided additional information on the proposed down select strategy, stating:

> The Navy remains committed to a 55 ship LCS program and intends to procure these ships through an acquisition strategy that leverages competition, fixed price contracting and stability in order to meet our overarching objectives of performance and affordability.
>
> In the best interest of the Government, the Navy cancelled the solicitation to procure up to three LCS Flight 0+ ships in FY10 due to affordability.
>
> Based on proposals received in August, the Navy had no reasonable basis to find that the LCS Program would be executable going forward under the current acquisition strategy, given the expectation of constrained budgets.
>
> In the near future, and working closely with Congress, the Navy will issue a new FY10 solicitation which downselects between the two existing designs and calls for building two ships in FY10 and provides options for two additional ships per year from FY11 to FY14 for a total of ten ships. The intent is for all of these ships to be built in one shipyard, which will benefit from a stable order quantity, training and production efficiencies to drive costs down. Both industry teams will have the opportunity to submit proposals for the FY10 ships under the new solicitation.
>
> To sustain competition throughout the life of the program and in conjunction with the downselect, the Navy will develop a complete Technical Data Package which will be used to open competition for a second source of the selected design in FY12, awarding one ship with options for up to four additional ships through FY14, to a new shipbuilder.
>
> Our FY10 solicitation will call for the prime to build an additional five combat systems to be delivered as government-furnished equipment for this second source shipyard. Separating the ship and combat systems procurement will enable bringing the LCS combat system into the broader Navy's open architecture plan.
>
> In short, this strategy calls for two shipbuilders in continuous competition for a single LCS seaframe design, and a government-provided combat system.
>
> The revised strategy meets the full spirit and intent of the Weapon Systems Acquisition Reform Act of 2009 by increasing Government oversight, employing fixed price contract types, maximizing competition, leveraging open architecture, using Economic Order Quantity and Block Buy strategies, and ensuring future competition for shipbuilding as enabled by development of a Technical Data Package to solicit ships from a second shipyard.
>
> We also continue to work closely with Congress on the Navy's LCS procurement intentions....
>
> The Navy intends to continue with construction and delivery of LCS 3 and LCS 4, ultimately for use as deployable assets. We will continue to explore all avenues to ensure this is an affordable program.[100]

---

[99] Department of Defense, "Littoral Combat Ship Down Select Announced," News Release 722-09, September 16, 2009, available online at http://www.defenselink mil/releases/release.aspx?releaseid=12984.

The Navy briefed CRS and CBO about the proposed down select strategy on September 22, 2009. Points made by the Navy in the briefing included the following:

- The bids from the two industry teams for the three LCSs requested in the FY2010 budget (which were submitted to the Navy in late July or early August 2009)[101] were above the LCS unit procurement cost cap in "all scenarios."

- Negotiations with the industry teams were deemed by the Navy to be not likely to result in award prices for the FY2010 ships that were acceptable to the Navy.

- The Navy judged that the current LCS teaming arrangements "considerably influenced costs" in the FY2010 bids.

- The Navy judged that it cannot afford more than a two-ship award in FY2010 within the amount of funding ($1,380 million) requested for LCS sea frame procurement in FY2010.

- In response to the above points, the Navy decided to seek a new acquisition strategy for LCSs procured in FY2010 and subsequent years that would make the LCS program affordable by leveraging competition, providing stability to LCS shipyards and suppliers, producing LCSs at efficient rates, giving industry incentives to make investments that would reduce LCS production costs, and increasing commonality in the resulting LCS fleet.

- Under the Navy's proposed strategy, the winner of the LCS down select would be awarded a contract to build two ships procured in FY2010, with options to build two more ships per year in FY2011-FY2014. The contract would be a block-buy contract augmented with Economic Order Quantity (EOQ) authority, so as to permit up-front batch purchases of long leadtime components, as would be the case under a multiyear procurement (MYP) contract. Unlike an MYP contract, however, the block buy contract would not include a termination liability.

- The winner of the down select would deliver to the Navy a technical data package that would permit another shipyard to build the winning LCS design.

- The Navy would hold a second competition to select a second LCS bidder. This competition would be open to all firms other than the shipyard that is building the 10 LCSs in FY2010-FY2014. The winner of this second competition would be awarded a contract to build up to five LCSs in FY2012-FY2014 (one ship in FY2012, and two ships per year in FY2013-FY2014).

- The Navy would maintain competition between the two shipyards for LCSs procured in FY2015 and subsequent years.

- The prime contactor on the team that wins the LCS down select (i.e., Lockheed or General Dynamics) would provide the combat systems for all the LCSs to be

---

(...continued)

[100] Email from Navy Office of Legislative Affairs to CRS, entitled "LCS Way Ahead," September 16, 2009.

[101] See, for example, Christopher P. Cavas, "LCS Bids Submitted to U.S. Navy," *DefenseNews.com*, August 3, 2009, which states: "Lockheed Martin announced its proposal was sent to the Navy on July 31, and rival General Dynamics confirmed its plans were sent in by the Aug. 3 deadline." See also Bettina H. Chavanne, "Lockheed Submits First LCS Proposal Under Cost Cap Regulations," *Aerospace Daily & Defense Report*, August 4, 2009: 5.

procured in FY2010-FY2014—the 10 that would be built by the first shipyard, and the others that would be built by the second shipyard.

- The structure of the industry team that wins the down select would be altered, with the prime contractor on the team being separated from the shipyard (i.e., the shipyard building the 10 LCSs in FY2010-FY2014). The separation, which would occur some time between FY2010 and FY2014, would be intended in part to prevent an organizational conflict of interest on the part of the prime contractor as it provides combat systems to the two shipyards building LCSs.

- The current combat system used on the selected LCS design will be modified over time to a configuration that increases its commonality with one or more of the Navy's existing surface ship combat systems.

- The Navy intends to complete the construction and delivery of LCS-3 and LCS-4.

- The Navy believes that the proposed acquisition strategy does the following: maximize the use of competition in awarding contracts for LCSs procured in FY2010-FY2014; provide an opportunity for achieving EOQ savings with vendors; provide stability and efficient production quantities to the shipyards and vendors; provide an opportunity to move to a common combat system for the LCS fleet; and provide the lowest-possible total ownership cost for the Navy for the resulting LCS fleet, in large part because the fleet would consist primarily of a single LCS design with a single logistics support system. The Navy also believes the proposed strategy is consistent with the spirit and intent of the Weapon Systems Acquisition Reform Act of 2009 (S. 454/P.L. 111-23 of May 22, 2009).

Regarding the Navy's ability to sustain a competition between two LCS builders for LCS construction contracts years from now, when the annual LCS procurement rate is projected to drop to 1.5 ships per year (i.e., a 1-2-1-2 pattern), Under Secretary of the Navy Robert Work reportedly stated:

> "We are going to be able to compete those. We will be able to compete three [ships] every two years and one of the yards will win two and one yard will win one. Sometimes, we'll do a five multi-year [procurement contract]. We have all sorts of flexibility in here," he said.[102]

Potential Oversight Questions for Congress

Prior to the Navy's November 3, 2010, proposal for a dual-award acquisition strategy, the proposed down select strategy posed several potential oversight questions for Congress, including the following:

- Did the timing of the Navy's September 2009 announcement of the strategy— very late in the congressional process for reviewing, marking up, and finalizing action on the FY2010 defense budget—provide Congress with sufficient time to

---

[102] Geoff Fein, "Official: Navy OK With Either LCS, New Acquisition Plan Adds Flexibility In Out Years," *Defense Daily*, February 18, 2010: 3.

adequately review the proposal prior to finalizing its action on the FY2010 defense budget?

- Does the Navy's proposed strategy allow the Navy enough time to adequately evaluate the operational characteristics of the two LCS designs before selecting one of those designs for all future production?

- Does the Navy's proposed method for conducting the LCS down select—the Request for Proposals (RFP)—appropriately balance procurement cost against other criteria, such as life-cycle operation and support (O&S) cost and ship capability?

- What risks would the Navy face if the shipyard that wins the competition to build the 10 LCSs in FY2010-FY2014 cannot build them within the contracted cost?

- How does the Navy plan to evolve the combat system on the winning LCS design to a configuration that has greater commonality with one or more existing Navy surface ship combat systems?

- What are the Navy's longer-term plans regarding the two "orphan" LCSs that are built to the design that is not chosen in the down select?

- What potential alternatives are there to this acquisition strategy?

Each of these questions is discussed briefly below.

Enough Time for Adequate Congressional Review of Navy Proposal?

One potential issue for Congress concerning the proposed down select strategy was whether the timing of the Navy's September 2009 announcement of the strategy—very late in the congressional process for reviewing, marking up, and finalizing action on the FY2010 defense budget—provided Congress with sufficient time to adequately review the proposal prior to finalizing its action on the FY2010 defense budget. The announcement of the Navy's proposed acquisition strategy on September 16, 2009, came

- after the defense committees of Congress had held their hearings to review the FY2010 budget submission;

- after the FY2010 defense authorization bill (H.R. 2647/S. 1390) and the DOD appropriations bill (H.R. 3326) had been reported in the House and Senate;

- after both the House and Senate had amended and passed their versions of the FY2010 defense authorization bill, setting the stage for the conference on that bill; and

- after the House had passed its version of the FY2010 DOD appropriations bill.

The timing of the Navy's announcement was a byproduct of the fact that the Navy was not able to see and evaluate the industry bids for the three LCSs that the Navy had originally requested for FY2010 until August 2009. The September 16, 2009, announcement date may have been the earliest possible announcement date, given the time the Navy needed to consider the situation created by the bids, evaluate potential courses of action, and select the proposed acquisition strategy.

Although the Navy might not have been able to present the proposed down select strategy to Congress any sooner than September 16, the timing of the Navy's announcement nevertheless put Congress in the position of being asked to approve a major proposal for the LCS program—a proposal that would determine the basic shape of the acquisition strategy for the program for many years into the future—with little or no opportunity for formal congressional review and consideration through hearings and committee markup activities.

A shortage of time for formal congressional review and consideration would be a potential oversight issue for Congress for any large weapon acquisition program, but this might have been especially the case for the LCS program, because it was not be the first time that the Navy put Congress in the position of having to make a significant decision about the LCS program with little or no opportunity for formal congressional review and consideration. As discussed in previous CRS reporting on the LCS program, a roughly similar situation occurred in the summer of 2002, after Congress had completed its budget-review hearings on the proposed FY2003 budget, when the Navy submitted a late request for the research and development funding that effectively started the LCS program.[103]

---

[103] The issue of whether Congress was given sufficient time to review and consider the merits of the LCS program in its early stages was discussed through multiple editions of past CRS reports covering the LCS program. The discussion in those reports raised the question of whether "Navy officials adopted a rapid acquisition strategy for the LCS program in part to limit the amount of time available to Congress to assess the merits of the LCS program and thereby effectively rush Congress into approving the start of LCS procurement before Congress fully understands the details of the program." The discussion continued:

> With regard to the possibility of rushing Congress into a quick decision on LCS procurement, it can be noted that announcing the LCS program in November 2001 and subsequently proposing to start procurement in FY2005 resulted in a situation of Congress having only three annual budget-review seasons to learn about the new LCS program, assess its merits against other competing DOD priorities, and make a decision on whether to approve the start of procurement. These three annual budget-review seasons would occur in 2002, 2003, and 2004, when Congress would review the Navy's proposed FY2003, FY2004, and FY2005 budgets, respectively. Congress' opportunity to conduct a thorough review of the LCS program in the first two of these three years, moreover, may have been hampered:
>
> • **2002 budget-review season (for FY2003 budget).** The Navy's original FY2003 budget request, submitted to Congress in February 2002, contained no apparent funding for development of the LCS. In addition, the Navy in early 2002 had not yet announced that it intended to employ a rapid acquisition strategy for the LCS program. As a result, in the early months of 2002, there may have been little reason within Congress to view the LCS program as a significant FY2003 budget-review issue. In the middle of 2002, the Navy submitted an amended request asking for $33 million in FY2003 development funding for the LCS program. Navy officials explained that they did not decide until the middle of 2002 that they wanted to pursue a rapid acquisition strategy for the LCS program, and consequently did not realize until then that there was a need to request $33 million in FY2003 funding for the program. By the middle of 2002, however, the House and Senate Armed Services committees had already held their spring FY2003 budget-review hearings and marked up their respective versions of the FY2003 defense authorization bill. These two committees thus did not have an opportunity to use the spring 2002 budget-review season to review in detail the Navy's accelerated acquisition plan for the LCS program or the supporting request for $33 million in funding.
>
> • **2003 budget-review season (for FY2004 budget).** To support a more informed review of the LCS program during the spring 2003 budget-review season, the conferees on the FY2003 defense authorization bill included a provision (Section 218) requiring the Navy to submit a detailed report on several aspects of the LCS program, including its acquisition strategy. In response to this legislation, the Navy in February 2003 submitted a report of eight pages in length, including a title page and a first page devoted mostly to a restatement of Section 218's requirement for the report. The House and Senate Armed Services committees, in their reports

(continued...)

Supporters of the idea of approving the Navy's proposed down select strategy as part of Congress's work to finalize action on the FY2010 defense budget could argue one or more of the following:

- The timing of the Navy's proposal, though not convenient for Congress, nevertheless represented a good-faith effort by the Navy to present the proposal to Congress at the earliest possible date. The Navy conducted multiple briefings with congressional offices starting in September 2009 to explain the proposed strategy.

- The LCS program needed to be put on a more stable long-term path as soon as possible, and if Congress did not approve the proposal as part of its work in finalizing action on the FY2010 defense budget, another year would pass before the LCS program could be put on a stable path approved by Congress.

- Although cost growth and construction problems with the LCS program can be viewed as a consequence of past attempts to move ahead too quickly on the LCS program, the Navy's acquisition strategy does not risk repeating this experience, because it does not represent another attempt to move ahead on the program at an imprudent speed. To the contrary, the strategy seeks to reduce execution risks by limiting LCS procurement to a maximum of four ships per year and providing a stable planning environment for LCS shipyards and suppliers.

- If the proposed strategy were not approved by Congress as part of its action on the FY2010 budget, the LCSs procured in FY2010 would be more expensive to procure, since they would not benefit from economies of scale that would come from awarding the FY2010 ships as part of a contract that also includes LCSs to be procured in FY2011-FY2014.

Supporters of the idea of deferring a decision on the Navy's proposed down select strategy until the FY2011 budget cycle could argue one or more of the following:

- Navy briefings to Congress on the proposed strategy starting in September 2009, though helpful, were not sufficient for Congress to fully understand the features and potential implications of the Navy's proposed acquisition strategy—much less the relative merits of potential alternatives to that strategy.

- The risks of making a quick decision on the Navy's proposed acquisition strategy, with little time for formal congressional review and consideration, are underscored by the history of the LCS program, which includes substantial cost growth and construction problems that can be viewed as the consequence of past

---

(...continued)

on the FY2004 defense authorization bill, have expressed dissatisfaction with the thoroughness of the report as a response to the requirements of Section 218. (For details, see the "Legislative Activity" section of this report.) It is thus not clear whether the defense authorization committees were able to conduct their spring 2003 budget-review hearings on the FY2004 budget with as much information about the LCS program as they might have preferred.

(See, for example, CRS Report RL 32109, *Na▢y DD▢▢▢▢▢ ▢▢▢an▢ ▢▢▢ ▢ip Ac▢isition ▢ro▢rams▢▢▢ersi▢▢t ▢ss▢es an▢▢ptions for ▢on▢ress*, by Ronald O'Rourke, updated July 29, 2005, pp. CRS-59 to CRS-60. This discussion was carried through multiple updates of CRS reports covering the LCS program.)

attempts to move ahead quickly on the program, without more-extensive congressional review and consideration.

- The desire to avoid paying a relatively high cost for LCSs procured in FY2010, though real, should not have been a controlling factor in this situation (i.e., should not have been "the tail that wags the dog"). Paying a higher cost for LCSs procured in FY2010, though not optimal, would be an investment to buy time for Congress to more fully review and consider the merits of both the Navy's proposal and potential alternatives to it. Problems avoided through a full congressional review and consideration of the Navy's proposal and potential alternatives during the FY2011 budget cycle could eventually save the Navy a lot more money than the Navy hopes to save on the LCSs procured in FY2010 by procuring them as part of a contract that also includes LCSs to be procured in FY2011-FY2014.

- Approving the Navy's proposed acquisition strategy at a late juncture in the annual congressional process for reviewing and marking up the defense budget would set an undesirable precedent from Congress's standpoint regarding late submissions to Congress of significant proposals for large defense acquisition programs, and encourage DOD to do the same with other large weapon acquisition programs in the future in the hopes of stampeding Congress into making quick decisions on major proposals for those programs.

Enough Time to Evaluate the Two Designs' Operational Characteristics?

Another potential issue for Congress concerning the Navy's down select strategy was whether the strategy allowed the Navy enough time to adequately evaluate the operational characteristics of the two LCS designs before selecting one of those designs for all future production. Potential oversight questions for Congress included the following:

- Since LCS-1 as of September 2009 had been in commissioned service for less than a year, and LCS-2 as of that date had not yet been delivered to the Navy, how firm was the basis for the Navy's determination that both LCS designs meet the Navy's operational requirements for LCS?

- By the summer of 2010—when the Navy plans to award a contract to the winner of the down select—the Navy will have had only a limited time to evaluate the operational characteristics of LCS-1 and LCS-2 through fleet exercises and use in actual Navy deployments. Will the Navy at that point have a sufficient understanding of the two designs' operational characteristics to appropriately treat the operational characteristics of the two designs in the down select?

The Navy and its supporters could argue that the Navy has chosen a preferred design for other new Navy ships (such as the DDG-1000 destroyer) on the basis of paper designs only, and consequently that the Navy would have a firmer basis for performing the LCS down select than it has had on other shipbuilding programs. They can argue that the Navy has a good understanding of the basic differences between the ships—that the Lockheed design, for example, may have better features for supporting small boat operations (which are used for certain LCS missions), while the General Dynamics design may have better features for supporting helicopter and unmanned aerial vehicle (UAV) operations (which are used for certain LCS missions).

Skeptics could argue that the Navy in the past has talked about performing an extensive operational review of each design prior to settling on an acquisition strategy for follow-on ships in the program, and that the innovative nature of the LCS—a modular ship with plug-and-fight mission packages and a small crew—increases the risks associated with selecting a single LCS design before performing such an extensive operational review. Skeptics could argue that the Navy is depriving itself of the opportunity to better understand, through exercises and real-world deployments, the implications for overall fleet operations of building all LCSs to one design or the other before performing the down select.

Weight Given to Procurement Cost vs. Other Factors in Request for Proposals (RFP)

Another potential issue for Congress concerning the Navy's down select strategy concerned the criteria that the Navy will use for selecting a winning design in the down select. Some observers, particularly supporters of the General Dynamics LCS design, argued that the Navy's proposed method for evaluating the two LCS designs in the LCS down select—set forth in the Request for Proposals (RFP) for the down select—focused too much on procurement cost and not enough on other factors, particularly life-cycle fuel cost, other components of life-cycle operating and support (O&S) cost, and ship capability. Other observers, particularly supporters of the Lockheed LCS design, argued (as did the Navy) that the Navy's proposed method for conducting the LCS down select adequately took into account factors other than procurement cost. The issue was viewed as having the potential for leading to a protest of the Navy's down select decision by the firm that is not selected.[104]

Regarding the role of life-cycle operation and support (O&S) cost in the Navy's down select decision, a February 2010 GAO report stated:

> The Navy estimated operating and support costs for LCS seaframes and mission packages in 2009, but the estimates do not fully reflect DOD and GAO best practices for cost estimating and may change due to program uncertainties. GAO's analysis of the Navy's 2009 estimates showed that the operating and support costs for seaframes and mission packages could total $84 billion (in constant fiscal year 2009 dollars) through about 2050. However, the Navy did not follow some best practices for developing an estimate such as (1) analyzing the likelihood that the costs could be greater than estimated, (2) fully assessing how the estimate may change as key assumptions change, and (3) requesting an independent estimate and comparing it with the program estimate. The estimates may also be affected by program uncertainties, such as potential changes to force structure that could alter the number of ships and mission packages required. The costs to operate and support a weapon system can total 70 percent of a system's costs, and the lack of an estimate that fully reflects best practices

---

[104] For examples of articles discussing this issue, see Sean Reilly, "Loser To Fight In LCS Deal?" *o ile A ress Re ister*, March 28, 2010: 1; Cid Standifer, "Austal USA, GD Officials Criticize Navy's RFP Criteria For LCS Award," *nsi e t e Na y*, March 29, 2010; Zachary M. Peterson, "Navy LCS Proposal Request Seeks 'Qualitative' Total Ownership Cost Figures," *nsi e t e Na y*, March 22, 2010; Emelie Rutherford, "Navy Stands By LCS Due Date As Hill Backers Of Each Bidder Swap Barbs," *Defense Daily*, March 18, 2010: 2-3; Geoff Fein, "General Dynamics' LCS Burns Less Fuel At Higher Speeds, Navy Documents Show," *Defense Daily*, March 2, 2010: 1-2; Geoff Fein, "Sessions Presses Navy Over Fairness of LCS RFP Evaluation," *Defense Daily*, March 1, 2010: 6-7; Geoff Fein, "USS Independence [LCS-2] Is The More Fuel Efficient of Two LCS Variants, Austal Official Says," *Defense Daily*, February 24, 2010: 2-3; Geoff Fein, "LCS RFP: Greater Emphasis Placed On Ship Price, Less On Life-Cycle Cost," *Defense Daily*, January 29, 2010: 5-7; Christopher P. Cavas, "RFP for LCS: Cost Main Factor in Winning Bid," *Na y imes.com*, January 28, 2010.

could limit decision makers' ability to identify the resources that will be needed over the long term to support the planned investment in LCS force structure. With a decision pending in 2010 on which seaframe to buy for the remainder of the program, decision makers could lack critical information to assess the full costs of the alternatives.[105]

A February 8, 2010, press report stated that "the Navy will draw up total life-cycle cost estimates for both the Lockheed Martin and General Dynamics versions of the Littoral Combat Ship before the program goes before the Defense Acquisition Board this year for its Milestone B. review. The service included the announcement in a response to a Government Accountability Office report that criticized LCS life-cycle estimates."[106]

At the request of Senator Jeff Sessions, the CBO analyzed the impact of O&S cost and other types of costs on the total life-cycle costs of the LCS and (for purposes of comparison) four other types of Navy ships. The results of CBO's analysis were released in the form of an April 28, 2010, letter to Senator Sessions. The letter states:

> CBO projected the life-cycle cost of the LCS-1 under three different assumptions about the average annual amount of fuel the ship will use over its 25-year life: low, moderate, and high. In all three scenarios, procurement costs dominate the life-cycle cost of the LCS-1, ranging from 58 percent to 66 percent of the total.... Personnel costs make up 14 percent to 16 percent of the LCS-1's total life-cycle cost in the various scenarios, and fuel costs account for 8 percent to 18 percent.
>
> The low-fuel case assumes that the LCS-1 generally operates at relatively low speeds—10 knots or less 90 percent of the time it is under way and 30 knots or more only about 3 percent of the time. That speed profile is based in part on how the Navy operated the LCS-1 between March 2009 and March 2010. In that scenario, operation and support costs total 33 percent of the ship's life-cycle cost: 16 percent for personnel costs, 8 percent for fuel costs (assuming that the ship consumes 25,000 barrels of fuel per year), and 9 percent for other O&S costs....
>
> The moderate-fuel case—which CBO considers the most likely of the three scenarios—assumes that the LCS-1 operates at 30 or more knots for about 5 percent of the time, at 14 knots to 16 knots 42 percent of the time (a range that might be typical when the ship was traveling from its home port to a deployment location), and at less than 12 knots for the rest of its time under way. In that scenario, O&S costs total 34 percent of the ship's life-cycle cost: 15 percent for personnel, 11 percent for fuel, and 8 percent for other O&S costs. The moderate speed profile would result in fuel usage of about 35,000 barrels per year, slightly less than the 37,600 barrels that the Navy assumed in formulating its 2011 budget request. By comparison, the [Navy's] FFG-7 class frigates consumed about 31,000 barrels of fuel per ship in 2009.
>
> The high-fuel case assumes that the LCS-1 operates at 30 or more knots for about 20 percent of its time under way, an assumption based partly on a speed profile developed by the Naval Sea Systems Command for the LCS program. In that scenario, O&S costs represent about 40 percent of the ship's life-cycle cost—more than in the other scenarios for the LCS-1 but less than for any of the other types of ships considered in this analysis. Personnel costs make up 14 percent of the life-cycle total; fuel costs, 18 percent; and other O&S costs, 8 percent.

[105] Government Accountability Office, *ittoral om at ip Actions Nee e to mpro e peratin ost stimates an iti ate Ris s in mplementin New oncepts*, GAO-10-257, February 2010, summary page.

[106] Cid Standifer, "Navy Will Project Operation Costs Of Both LCS Models for DAB Review," *nsi e t e Na y*, February 8, 2010.

Projected fuel usage in this scenario is about 67,000 barrels per year. That estimate is unlikely to be exceeded in actual practice: It is twice the historical average for frigates and about 80 percent of the amount used by the Navy's destroyers (which do not have the capability to speed at 40 knots, as the littoral combat ship does, but are three times larger than the LCS-1).[107]

At a May 6, 2010, hearing on Navy shipbuilding programs before the Seapower Subcommittee of the Senate Armed Services Committee, Senator Sessions questioned Sean Stackley, the Navy's acquisition executive (i.e., the Assistant Secretary of the Navy [Research, Development and Acquisition]), regarding the role of fuel costs in the Navy's evaluation of the two LCS designs.

Potential Risks If First Shipyard Cannot Build Ships Within Cost

Another potential issue for Congress concerning the Navy's down select strategy concerned the potential risks the Navy would face if the shipyard that wins the competition to build the 10 LCSs in FY2010-FY2014 cannot build them within the contracted cost. The competition between the two existing LCS industry teams to be the winner of the down select could be intense enough to encourage the teams to bid unrealistically low prices for the contract to build the 10 ships.

The Navy and its supporters could argue that the Navy's plan to award a fixed-price contract to the winner of the down select would shift the cost risk on the 10 ships from the government to the shipyard. They could also argue that the Navy plans to carefully evaluate the bid prices submitted by the two industry teams for the down select to ensure that they are realistic, and that the existence of the second LCS shipyard would provide the Navy with an ability to continue building LCSs if production at the first yard were disrupted due to financial issues.

Skeptics could argue that even with a fixed-price contract, the Navy's proposed strategy poses cost risks for the government, because a shipyard could submit an unrealistically low bid so as to win the down select, and then recover its losses on those 10 ships by rolling the losses into prices for downstream ships in the program. Alternatively, the shipyard could present the Navy with the prospect of going out of business and disrupting the LCS production effort unless the Navy were to provide a financial bailout to cover the yard's losses on the 10 ships. Skeptics could argue that Navy decisions dating back to the 1970s to award multi-ship construction contracts to shipyards that had not yet built many ships of the kind in question sometimes led to less-than-satisfactory program outcomes, including substantial financial bailouts.

Increasing LCS Combat System Commonality with Other Combat Systems

Another potential issue for Congress regarding the Navy's down select strategy concerned the Navy's plan to evolve the combat system on the winning LCS design to a configuration that has greater commonality with one or more existing Navy surface ship combat systems. The Navy in its September 16, 2009, announcement did not provide many details on this part of its proposed acquisition strategy, making it difficult to evaluate the potential costs and risks of this part of the strategy against potential alternatives, including an alternative (which Navy officials have discussed in the past) of designing a new LCS combat system that would, from the outset, be highly common with one or more existing Navy surface ship combat systems.

---

[107] Letter dated April 28, 2010, from Douglas W. Elmendorf, Director, CBO, to the Honorable Jeff Sessions, pp. 3-5. The letter is available online at http://www.cbo.gov/ftpdocs/114xx/doc11431/04-28-SessionsLetter.pdf.

Navy's Longer-Term Plans Regarding Two "Orphan" Ships

Another potential issue for Congress concerning the Navy's down select strategy concerned the Navy's longer-term plans regarding the two "orphan" LCSs built to the design that was not selected in the down select. The Navy stated that it planned to keep these two ships in the fleet because they will be capable ships and the Navy has an urgent need for LCSs. These two LCSs, however, will have unique logistic support needs, potentially making them relatively expensive to operate and support. At some point, as larger numbers of LCSs enter service, the costs of operating and supporting these two ships may begin to outweigh the increasingly marginal addition they make to total LCS fleet capabilities. Potential alternatives to keeping the ships in the active-duty fleet as deployable assets include selling them to foreign buyers, converting them into research and development platforms, shifting them to the Naval Reserve Force (where they would be operated by crews consisting partially of reservists), or decommissioning them and placing them into preservation (i.e., "mothball") status as potential mobilization assets. Potential questions for Congress included the following:

- Does the Navy intend to keep the two orphan LCSs in the active-duty fleet as deployable assets for a full 25-year service life?

- If so, how would be the life-cycle operation and support (O&S) costs of these two ships compare to those of the other LCSs? In light of these O&S costs, would it be cost-effective to keep these two ships in the active-duty fleet as deployable assets for a full 25-year service life, particularly as large numbers of LCSs enter service?

- If the Navy does not intend to keep the two orphan LCSs in the active-duty fleet as deployable assets for a full 25-year service life, when does the Navy anticipate removing them from such service, and what does the Navy anticipate doing with them afterward?

Potential Alternatives to Navy's September 2009 Strategy

Another potential issue for Congress concerning the Navy's down select strategy concerned potential alternatives to that strategy. A variety of alternatives can be generated by changing one or more elements of the Navy's proposed strategy. One alternative would be a strategy that would keep both LCS designs in production, at least for the time being. Such a strategy might involve the following:

- the use of block-buy contracts with augmented EOQ authority, as under the Navy's proposed acquisition strategy, to continue producing both LCS designs, so as to provide stability to shipyards and suppliers involved in producing both LCS designs;

- the use of Profit Related to Offer (PRO) bidding between the builders of the two LCS designs, so as to generate competitive pressure between them and thereby restrain LCS production costs;[108] and

---

[108] Under PRO bidding, the two shipyards would compete not for LCS quantities (because each shipyard would know that it was going to build a certain number of LCSs over the term of their block-buy contracts), but rather for profit, with the lowest bidder receiving the higher profit margin. PRO bidding has been used in other defense acquisition programs where bidders do not compete for quantity. The Navy, for example, began using PRO bidding in the DDG-51 (continued...)

- designing a new LCS combat system that would have a high degree of commonality with one or more existing Navy surface ship combat systems and be provided as government-furnished equipment (GFE) for use on both LCS designs—an idea that was considered by the Navy at an earlier point in the program.

The Navy's November 3, 2010, proposal for a dual-award LCS acquisition strategy is broadly similar to the notional dual-award approach outlined above. This notional dual-award approach has been presented in this CRS report as an option for Congress since September 27, 2009, when the report was updated to incorporate the Navy's September 16, 2009, announcement of its proposed down select strategy. The discussion below concerns the notional dual-award approach outlined above.

Supporters of an alternative like the one outlined above could argue that it would

- provide stability to LCS shipyards and suppliers;

- use competition to restrain LCS production costs;

- permit the Navy to receive a full return on the investment the Navy made in creating both LCS designs;

- reduce the life-cycle operation and support costs associated with building two LCS designs by equipping all LCSs with a common combat system;

- allow the Navy to design an LCS combat system that is, from the outset, highly common with one or more of the Navy's existing surface ship combat systems;

- achieve a maximum LCS procurement rate of four ships per year starting in FY2011 (two years earlier than under the Navy's proposal), thus permitting more LCSs to enter service with the Navy sooner;

- build both LCS designs in substantial numbers, thereby avoiding a situation of having a small number of orphan LCS ships that could have potentially high operation and support costs;

- preserve a potential to neck down to a single LCS design at some point in the future, while permitting the Navy in the meantime to more fully evaluate the operational characteristics of the two designs in real-world deployments; and

- increase the potential for achieving foreign sales of LCSs (which can reduce production costs for LCSs made for the U.S. Navy) by offering potential foreign buyers two LCS designs with active production lines.

Supporters of the Navy's proposed acquisition strategy could argue that an alternative like the one outlined above would, compared to the Navy's proposed strategy

- achieve lower economies of scale in LCS production costs by splitting production of LCS components between two designs;

(...continued)
destroyer program it in the 1990s.

- achieve, at the outset of series production of LCSs, less bidding pressure on shipyards, and thus higher LCS production costs, than would be achieved under the Navy's proposed strategy of using a price-based competition to select a single design for all future LCS production;

- miss out on the opportunity to restrain LCS costs by using the level of efficiency achieved in building an LCS design at one shipyard as a directly applicable benchmark for gauging the level of efficiency achieved by the other shipyard in building the same LCS design;

- increase Navy LCS program-management costs and the burden on Navy program-management capabilities by requiring the Navy to continue managing the construction of two very different LCS designs;

- achieve lower economies of scale in LCS operation and support costs because the two LCS designs would still differ in their basic hull, mechanical, and electrical (HM&E) systems, requiring the Navy to maintain two separate HM&E logistics support systems;

- receive only a limited return on the investment the Navy made in developing the two current LCS combat systems (since LCSs in the long run would not use either one), and require the Navy to incur the costs and the technical risks associated with designing a completely new LCS combat system;

- require the Navy to build some number of LCSs with their current combat systems—which are different from one another and from other Navy surface ship combat systems—while awaiting the development of the new LCS combat system, and then incur the costs associated with backfitting these earlier LCSs with the new system when it becomes available;

- send to industry a signal that is undesirable from the government's perspective that if the Navy or other parts or DOD begin producing two designs for a new kind of weapon system, the Navy or DOD would be reluctant to neck production down to a single design at some point, even if government believes that doing so would reduce program costs while still meeting operational objectives; and

- miss out on the opportunity that would be present under the Navy's proposed acquisition strategy to increase the potential for achieving foreign sales of LCSs by offering potential foreign buyers an LCS design that, through U.S. production, enjoys significant economies of scale for both production and operation and support.

Appendix D. Dual-Award Acquisition Strategy Announced in November 2010

This appendix presents additional background information on the dual-award acquisition strategy announced by the Navy on November 3, 2009.

November 4, 2010, Navy Point Paper

A November 4, 2010, Navy point paper on the dual-award strategy proposed on November 3, 2010, stated the following (this is the full text of the point paper):[109]

Littoral Combat Ship Proposed Revised Acquisition

Dual Ten Ship Awards

- In summer 2009 Navy received bids for three FY10 ships from Lockheed Martin/Marinette Marine/Bollinger and General Dynamics Bath Iron Works/Austal USA industry teams. These bids did not reflect competitive pricing and well exceeded the Congressional Cost Cap. In order to reverse cost trends on the program, the acquisition strategy was revised to the current down select strategy.

- The Navy's Littoral Combat Ship acquisition strategy to down select to a single design has resulted in a highly effective competition between the industry bidders. Navy is on the path to down select in accordance with the terms of the current solicitation.

- The industry response to the competitive acquisition strategy has resulted in has resulted in reduction in cost for the LCS ships relative to the previous bids. These competitive bids, coupled with Navy's desires to increase ship procurement rates to support operational requirements, has created an opportunity to award each bidder a fixed price ten-ship block buy—a total of 20 ships from Fiscal Year 2010 to Fiscal Year 2015. A comparison between the two strategies of which ships are included in a down select/second source versus dual 10 ship block buy appears in the table below.

- The current NDAA [national defense authorization act] language permits the Navy to procure up to 10 ships in a block buy. In order to execute a dual ten ship award, Navy believes Congressional authorization is required.

- If Congressional support for this approach is granted, Navy will work with industry to revise the ship procurement schedules within current proposal pricing (FY10 – FY15 vice FY10 – FY14).

- Navy is continuing on the path to down select and absent authorization, we will proceed to down select by mid-December 2010.

- There are numerous benefits to this approach including stabilizing the LCS program and the industrial base with award of 20 ships; increasing ship procurement rate to support

---

[109] Source: Navy point paper on proposed alternative LCS acquisition strategy dated November 4, 2010.

operational requirements; sustaining competition through the program; and enhancing Foreign Military Sales opportunities.

- The Navy intends to procure the Technical Data Package for both designs and if necessary a second source for either or both designs could be brought into the program.

- Either approach will ensure the Navy procures affordably priced ships.

		FY10	FY11	FY12	FY13	FY14	FY15	TOTAL
Downselect	Winner	2	2	2	2	2	4	19
	Second Source			1	2	2		
	TOTAL	2	2	3	4	4	4	
Dual Award	Contractor A	1	1	2	2	2	2	20
	Contractor B	1	1	2	2	2	2	
	TOTAL	2	2	4	4	4	4	

Near-Term Issue for Congress

The Navy's proposed dual-award strategy posed a near-term issue for Congress of whether this strategy would be preferable to the down select strategy, and whether Congress should grant the Navy, by December 30, the additional legislative authority the Navy would need to implement the dual-award strategy.

December 14 Senate Armed Services Committee Hearing

On December 14, 2010, the Senate Armed Services Committee held a hearing to review the Navy's proposed dual-award strategy. The witnesses at the hearing included Navy leaders and representatives from CBO, GAO, and CRS. The committee's web page for the hearing[110] contains links to the prepared statements of the GAO and CRS witnesses, and states that the Navy and CBO witnesses did not submit their prepared statements in electronic form. (The CBO witness asked in his opening remarks that CBO's December 10, 2010, letter report on the relative costs of the down select and dual-award strategies[111] be entered into the record for the hearing. CBO's letter report is available from the CBO website.) The committee's web page for the hearing also contains a link to the transcript of the hearing.

Some General Observations

General observations that could be made on the Navy's proposed dual-award strategy included but are not limited to the following:

---

[110] http://armed-services.senate.gov/testimony.cfm?wit_id=9812&id=4897.

[111] Congressional Budget Office, letter report to Senator John McCain on LCS acquisition strategies dated December 10, 2010, 7 pp.

- The dual-award strategy would avoid, at least for now, the possibility of a contract protest being filed against a Navy down select decision.

- Although the dual-award strategy includes the possibility of the Navy at some point bringing a second source into the program for either or both LCS designs, the dual-award strategy does not include the guaranteed opportunity present in the down select strategy for shipyards not currently involved in building LCSs to compete for the right to become the second LCS builder.

- The Navy's November 4, 2010, point paper on the dual-award strategy does not outline the Navy's intentions regarding the currently different combat systems (i.e., the built-in collections of sensors, weapons, displays, and software) on the two LCS designs.

- The dual-award strategy would require each LCS contractor to build 10 ships over a period of six years (FY2010-FY2015) rather than five years (FY2010-FY2014), but at the same price that was bid for the five-year schedule. In addition, LCSs built under the dual-award strategy would incorporate combat systems that would be built by combat system manufacturers in smaller annual quantities than would be the case under the down select strategy, possibly increasing the costs of these combat systems. Factors such as these could, at the margin, alter the profitability for each contractor of building its respective group of 10 ships.

It could also be noted that the Navy's proposed dual-award strategy is broadly similar to a notional dual-award approach that was presented in this CRS report as an option for Congress (see **Appendix C**) since September 27, 2009, when the report was updated to incorporate the Navy's September 16, 2009, announcement of its proposed down select strategy.

Potential Oversight Questions for Congress

Potential oversight questions for Congress in assessing whether the proposed dual-award strategy would be preferable to the down select strategy, and whether to grant the Navy, by December 30, the additional legislative authority the Navy would need to implement a dual-award strategy, included but were not limited to the following:

- Did the timing of the Navy's proposal provide Congress with enough time to adequately assess the relative merits of the down select strategy and the dual-award strategy? Given that the contractors submitted their bids by about September 15, could the Navy have notified Congress of the proposed dual-award strategy sooner than November 3, giving Congress more time to seek information on and evaluate the proposal? Should the Navy have asked the contractors to extend their bid prices for another, say, 30 or 60 or 90 days beyond the original December 14 expiration date, so as to provide more time for congressional review of the Navy's proposal?[112] (As mentioned earlier, on

---

[112] A December 6, 2010, press report states: "Lockheed officials have indicated that they could extend the pricing in their proposal for a short while beyond Dec. 14, to allow time for Congress to approve the change. Lockheed Chief Financial Officer Bruce Tanner told an investment conference last week that Lockheed could extend the prices it offered for a day or two, but not indefinitely.... Analysts said they expected both companies to show some flexibility on the expiration of their pricing, given that each firm stood to win a contract valued at around $5 billion." (Andrea (continued...)

December 13, it was reported that the two LCS bidders, at the Navy's request, had extended the prices in their bids for 16 days, to December 30. At the December 14 hearing, Navy witnesses expressed strong doubts about the willingness of the bidders to extend their bid prices for any significant additional amount of time, since agreements with their parts suppliers and other arrangements on which the bids are based would no longer be valid.)

- What role, if any, did a desire by the Navy to avoid a potential contract protest against the Navy's down select decision play in the Navy's decision to propose the alternate dual-award strategy? For example, how concerned, if at all, was the Navy that the announcement of an LCS down select decision might lead to a contract protest and controversy somewhat like what has been experienced in the Air Force's KC-X aerial refueling tanker acquisition program?[113] A December 13, 2010, press report on the LCS program stated: "One high-level Navy source recently said that without the dual-ship approach, 'there is 100 percent chance of a protest.'"[114]

- What are the potential relative costs of the down select and dual-award acquisition strategies, including development costs, procurement costs, and life-cycle operation and support (O&S) costs? Did the Navy fully and accurately estimated these costs—including potential costs for developing, procuring, and installing a common combat system for both LCS designs—and reported all these potential costs to Congress?

- What are the potential relative risks of the down select and dual-award acquisition strategies, including development risks, production cost risks, production schedule risks, and life-cycle O&S risks? Did the Navy fully and accurately estimated these risks, and reported all these potential risks to Congress?

- What are the Navy's intentions, under the proposed dual-award acquisition strategy, regarding the currently different combat systems on the two LCS designs? Does the Navy intend to leave them unchanged, adopt one of the combat systems as the common system for both designs, or develop a new combat system for both designs? If the Navy intends to pursue the second or third of these paths, what is the Navy's plan (including schedule) for doing so? If the Navy does not have a definite plan regarding the combat systems for the ships, how well can the potential costs and risks of the dual-award strategy be estimated and compared to those of the down select strategy?

- What are the potential industrial-base impacts of the dual-award strategy, including impacts on the two LCS contractors, on shipyards that could, under the

(...continued)

Shalal-Esa, "U.S. Navy Hopeful Congress Will Approve Ship Buys," *Reuters.com*, December 6, 2010.) Another December 6, 2010, press report that was posted online on December 3, 2010, stated: "Theoretically, Lockheed Martin and Austal could likely agree to extend the price deadline, but the Navy has not asked them to do so yet, [Navy spokeswoman Captain Cate] Mueller said." (Cid Standifer, "Stand-Alone Bill May Be Needed To Approve LCS Dual Block Buy Plan," *Inside the Navy*, December 6, 2010.)

[113] For more on the KC-X program, see CRS Report RL34398, *Air Force KC-X Tanker Aircraft Program*, by Jeremiah Gertler.

[114] Christopher P. Cavas, "Deadline Looms For U.S. Navy's LCS," *Defense News*, December 13, 2010: 1.

down select strategy, bid for the right to become the second LCS builder, and on combat system manufacturers?

- What impact, if any, might the Navy's proposal to shift from its down select strategy to the dual-award strategy have on the ability of the DOD to implement down select strategies for other acquisition programs? For example, will the Navy's proposal to shift to the dual-award strategy cause contractors bidding for other acquisition programs to treat with increased skepticism stated DOD intentions to carry out down selects? If so, could that reduce the benefits of competition that DOD might hope to achieve through the use of down select strategies?

Enough Time for Adequate Congressional Review of Navy Proposal?

Regarding whether the timing of the Navy's proposal provides Congress with enough time to adequately assess the relative merits of the down select strategy and the dual-award strategy, it can be noted that this was the third time in the history of the LCS program that the Navy presented Congress with an important choice about the future of the LCS program late in the congressional budget-review cycle, after Congress had completed its spring budget-review hearings and some of its committee markups. The first instance was in mid-2002, when the Navy submitted an amended request to Congress for FY2003 funding to get the LCS program started using a rapid acquisition strategy.[115] The second was in September 2009, when the Navy announced its proposed down select strategy for the LCS program (see the discussion of this issue in **Appendix C**).

In light of the third instance—the Navy's proposal of November 3, 2010, for using a dual-award strategy rather than a down select strategy—a potential issue for Congress are the implications for the LCS program and congressional oversight of defense acquisition programs in general of proceeding with the LCS program in part on the basis of policies originally presented as proposals to Congress late in the congressional budget-review cycle, after Congress had completed its spring budget-review hearings and some of its committee markups. The Navy's November 3, 2010, notification to Congress of the proposed dual-award strategy, combined with a request by the Navy that Congress act on that proposal by December 30, provided relatively little time for Congress to collect cost and other information from the Navy (including information that Navy might not offer in initial briefings to individual congressional offices), for Congress to solicit cost and other information from independent sources such as CBO and GAO,

---

[115] The Navy's original FY2003 budget request, submitted to Congress in February 2002, contained no apparent funding for development of the LCS. In addition, the Navy in early 2002 had not yet announced that it intended to employ a rapid acquisition strategy for the LCS program. As a result, in the early months of 2002, there may have been little reason within Congress to view the LCS program as a significant FY2003 budget-review issue. In the middle of 2002, the Navy submitted an amended request asking for $33 million in FY2003 development funding for the LCS program. Navy officials explained that they did not decide until the middle of 2002 that they wanted to pursue a rapid acquisition strategy for the LCS program, and consequently did not realize until then that there was a need to request $33 million in FY2003 funding for the program. By the middle of 2002, however, the House and Senate Armed Services committees had already held their spring FY2003 budget-review hearings and marked up their respective versions of the FY2003 defense authorization bill. These two committees thus did not have an opportunity to use the spring 2002 budget-review season to review in detail the Navy's accelerated acquisition plan for the LCS program or the supporting request for $33 million in funding.

---

for CBO and GAO to develop such information and provide it to Congress, for Congress to hold hearings at which all this information might be discussed in a group setting, with multiple parties present, and for congressional offices to then form their evaluations of the Navy's proposal.

Relative Costs

Regarding the relative costs of the down select and dual-award acquisition strategies, there were at least three significant cost elements to consider: ship procurement costs; costs for possibly modifying the combat systems on LCSs so as to achieve more commonality in combat system equipment among all LCSs, and between LCSs and other Navy ships; and operational and support (O&S) costs.

Ship Procurement Costs

Navy Estimate

Regarding ship procurement costs, the Navy estimates that procuring LCSs under the dual-award strategy would cost $1 billion less through ⬜⬜⬜⬜⬜, and $600 million less through ⬜⬜⬜⬜⬜, than procuring them under the down select strategy. The Navy states that the $1 billion in savings through FY2016 translates to $910 million in net present value terms, and that the $600 million in savings through FY2015 translates to $496 million in net present value terms.[116]

The Navy estimates that ship procurement costs will be lower under the dual-award strategy than they would have been under the down select strategy due to the following cost factors, which are not listed in any particular order:[117]

- **Costs due to the second source under down select strategy building its first LCS.** The Navy estimates that certain ship procurement costs would be higher under the down select strategy because the second source under the down select strategy—that is, the unknown shipyard that would have been chosen in the second-stage competition that would have occurred under the down select strategy—would be building its first LCS. These higher costs include the following:

  - **Tooling, jigs, fixtures, etc.** The second source under the down select strategy would incur costs for the purchase of LCS-specific tooling, jigs, fixtures, etc. Marinette and Austal have already paid for these things.

  - **Engineering and support services.** The Navy's estimate includes a higher cost for engineering and support services at the second source under the down select strategy, because these costs typically are higher for a lead ship at a shipyard than for subsequent ships at that yard.

  - **Learning curve position.** In estimating the amount of labor hours required to build the first ship covered under the second source's block-buy contract,

---

[116] Source for $496 million figure: Navy briefing to CRS and CBO, March 30, 2011.

[117] Source for these points: Navy information paper dated April 12, 2011, as clarified and elaborated in a telephone conversation with CRS on April 21, 2011.

the Navy's estimate takes into account the fact that the second source under the dual-award strategy has already built LCSs (i.e., the yard is already some way down its LCS production learning curve), whereas the second source under the down select strategy would be building its first LCS (i.e., the yard would be at the top of its LCS production learning curve).

- **Change orders.** The Navy budgets a 10% allowance for change orders (i.e., design changes) for a lead ship built at a shipyard, compared to 5% for subsequent ships built at that yard.

- **Rework.** The Navy's estimate includes a higher cost for rework at the second source under the down select strategy because lead ships typically experience higher rework rates.

- **Slope of shipyard learning curve.** The Navy estimates that the second source under the dual-award strategy will achieve a steeper production learning curve (i.e., a greater amount of ship-to-ship reduction in shipyard labor hours required to build each ship) than would have been achieved by the second source under the down select strategy. In making this estimate, the Navy cites facilities improvements at Marinette and Austal that the Navy believes will permit Marinette and Austal to achieve learning curves of a certain steepness.

- **Shipyard labor rates.** The Navy estimates that the second source under the dual-award strategy will feature labor rates that are lower than those that would have occurred at the second source under the down select strategy.

- **Vendor material costs.** The Navy estimates that the second source under the dual-award strategy will obtain lower material prices from vendors than the second source under the down select strategy would have obtained because the second source under the dual-award strategy can seek bids from vendors on materials for a 10-ship contract, while the second source under the down select strategy would have sought bids from vendors on materials for a 5-ship contract.[118]

- **Profit rates.** The Navy estimates that the profit rates earned by second source under the dual-award strategy are lower than those that would be earned by the second source under the down select strategy, due to aggressive bidding by Marinette and Austal during what these yards thought was the first-stage competition under the down select strategy—a competition that was to have chosen the one LCS design to which all future LCSs would be built.

In evaluating the Navy's treatment of the above cost factors, potential questions include the following:

- How reasonable is it for the Navy to estimate that the second source under the dual-award strategy would have a steeper shipyard learning curve, lower shipyard labor rates, and a lower profit rate than the second source under the down select strategy would have had? Given the number and capabilities of

---

[118] The Navy also adjusted its cost estimate to account for differences in production quantities of scale for LCS combat systems that would occur under the down select and dual-award strategies. Under the down select strategy, one combat system maker would make combat systems for all LCSs. Under the dual-award strategy, two combat system makers would each make combat systems for one-half of the LCSs.

shipyards that might have participated in the second stage competition under the down select strategy, the potential intensity of a competition among these yards to win a share of a large Navy shipbuilding program, and the uncertainty about which specific yard might have won that competition, how certain can the Navy be that the second source that was chosen under that competition would have a shallower learning curve (and that it would not make facility investments to achieve a steeper curve), higher labor costs, and a lower profit rate than the second source under the dual-award strategy?

- How reasonable is it for the Navy to estimate that the second source under the down select strategy would have higher vendor material costs, given that this second source might have been a builder of other Navy ships and consequently might have been able to bundle its LCS material purchases together with those for its other Navy ships, so as to achieve increased economies of scale in material production? Navy officials in recent years have encouraged shipyards to achieve cross-yard economies of scale of this kind.

- If the second source under the down select strategy were instead estimated to be equal to the second source under the dual-award strategy in terms of shipyard learning curve slope, shipyard labor rates, vendor material costs, and profit rates, how much would this reduce the Navy's estimate of the savings in ship procurement costs that would occur under the dual-award strategy?

CBO Estimate

In contrast to the Navy, which estimated that ship procurement costs would be lower under the dual-award strategy, CBO in its December 10, 2010, letter report estimated that ship procurement costs would be $740 million higher more through FY2015 under the dual-award strategy. CBO's letter report included several cautionary statements about its estimates relating to limits on the information available to CBO in developing its estimates. The Navy and CBO estimates of ship procurement costs through FY2015 are summarized in **Table D-1**.

Table D-1. Navy and CBO Estimates of Ship Procurement Costs Through FY2015 Under Down Select and Dual-Award Strategies

For the period FY2010-FY2015, in current (i.e., then-year) dollars

Acquisition approaches	Estimated Cost
Navy estimate	
19-ship down-select plan	10,400 million
20-ship dual-award plan	9,800 million
Difference between two plans	Dual-award plan costs $600 million *less*
CBO estimate	
19-ship down-select plan	11,080 million
20-ship dual-award plan	11,820 million
Difference between two plans	Dual-award plan costs $740 million *more*

Source: Table prepared by CRS based on data presented in Congressional Budget Office, letter report to Senator John McCain on LCS acquisition strategies dated December 10, 2010, Table 2 on page 5.

December 14, 2010, Hearing

At the December 14, 2010, hearing on LCS acquisition strategy before the Senate Armed Services Committee, the Navy witnesses defended the Navy's estimate, stating that it was based on actual bid data from the two LCS bidders, and that CBO's estimate did not reflect full exposure to these bid data, because the data were proprietary and were being closely held by the Navy pending a potential announcement by the Navy of a down select decision (if the dual-award strategy were not pursued).

As discussed in the previous section, however, the Navy's estimate was also based on certain assumptions about the unknown shipyard that would have been chosen under the second-stage competition that would have occurred under the down select strategy. The Navy's assumptions about this unknown yard compared to the second source under the dual-award strategy accounts for some portion of the Navy's estimated savings.

Potential Changes in Costs of Other Ships Not Accounted For

Under the down select strategy, shipyards competing to become the second LCS builder could include yards that currently build other ships for the Navy, such as, possibly, General Dynamics' Bath Iron Works (GD/BIW) of Bath, ME, Northrop Grumman's Ingalls shipyard of Pascagoula, MS, or General Dynamics' National Steel and Shipbuilding Company (NASSCO) of San Diego, CA. If such a yard were to be selected under the down select strategy to become the second LCS builder, it could reduce the cost of other Navy ships being built at that yard by more fully spreading the fixed overhead costs of that yard. The Navy and CBO estimates in **Table D-1** do not account for possible changes in the costs of other Navy ships that might be occur as a consequence of changes in the spreading of shipyard fixed overhead costs.

Combat System Modification Costs

Any savings the dual-award strategy might realize relative to the down select strategy in terms of costs for procuring LCSs could be offset by potential additional costs under the dual-award strategy for modifying the combat systems on LCSs so as to achieve more commonality in combat system equipment among all LCSs, and between LCSs and other Navy ships. Prior to its September 2009 announcement of its proposed down select strategy, Navy officials on some occasions had spoken about the possibility of modifying the combat systems of one or both LCS designs so as to achieve more commonality in combat system equipment among all LCSs, and between LCSs and other Navy ships.[119]

A November 29, 2010, press report stated that "the Navy intends to keep separate the combat systems of the Lockheed and Austal USA versions of the Littoral Combat Ships for its dual buy strategy, but will 'procure the tech data package to allow for consideration of [a] common combat system in the future,' according to Navy spokeswoman Capt. Cate Mueller." The report also quoted an industry official as saying that the Navy is likely "still strategizing as to how they're going to single up on a combat system."[120]

---

[119] See, for example, Christopher P. Cavas, "Two LCS Designs, One Big Dilemma," *Defense News*, December 13, 2010: 22.

[120] Andrew Burt, "Navy Open To Combining Combat Systems On Both Littoral Combat Ships," *Inside the Navy*, (continued...)

At the December 14 hearing, the Navy stated the following regarding the issue of potential combat system modification costs:

> The current [LCS] acquisition strategy does not call for the changeout of the [LCS] combat system.
>
> Let me describe some characteristics of the combat system. As it was mentioned earlier, the total cost for the [LCS] combat system is on the order of about $70 million. When we think of the combat system, we break it down into a couple key components—weapons, sensors, and command and control [aka command and decision, or C and D] system. We have in fact, on the weapons side of the combat system, commonality [between the two LCS designs]. Both ships' 57-millimeter Bofors guns, both ships we're looking at RAM–CRAM [sic: RAM or SEARAM] weapons systems. So the weapon system is already common both between them and also with other ships in the inventory.
>
> Now, on the sensor side, we have contemplated moving towards a common sensor, and inside of this solicitation the Navy asked for priced bids for a new sensor to consider for the future. In total, the cost for bringing a new sensor—that's both common for LCS and with the rest of the fleet—is about $20 million nonrecurring and about $2 million a ship difference.
>
> So weapons are common. If the Navy chose to go to a common system for performance reasons, the cost impact would be about $20 million nonrecurring and a couple million dollars a ship.
>
> Then on the C and D side, which is largely the software system and displays and processors, the Navy does not have a drive right now to go towards common C and D for this class either in the down-select or dual-award. It is something that we could consider in the future.[121]

A January 17, 2011, press report stated:

> "The median class size in the Navy is about 12 to 14 ships, so we have a lot of 12-ship classes that have their own combat system," [Rear Admiral David Lewis, the Navy's program executive officer for ships,] said, "so we have no plans on changing the combat system on the ships. They're effective. At this point, they meet the requirements, and so I don't see any appetite in the Navy for changing those."...
>
> Lewis admitted that the business case could change after the two 10-ship contracts have run their course, but said he was skeptical it would make more sense to change combat systems then than now.[122]

An August 18, 2011, press report stated:

> [Rear Admiral James] Murdoch [head of the program executive office], said the Navy has not yet decided on whether both classes should have the same combat system or whether the

---

(...continued)

November 29, 2010. Material in brackets as in original. The Austal USA version of the LCS is the version developed by the General Dynamics-led LCS industry team.

[121] Transcript of spoken testimony of Sean J. Stackley, Assistant Secretary of Navy for Research, Development, and Acquisition.

[122] Cid Standifer, "Rear Adm. Lewis: Navy Has 'No Appetite' To Change LCS Combat System," *Inside the Navy*, January 17, 2011.

---

program should shift to a single system. There was no timeframe for a decision and the Navy was awaiting feedback from the two firms, he said.

"I'm not going to prejudge that," he said, adding he did not expect any changes in the "immediate term."[123]

A March 17, 2013, press report states that "the Navy has been strongly considering a downselect to a single LCS combat system in 2015, doing away with one of the program's most glaring inefficiencies. Consideration of a downselect to a single design also has been underway."[124]

The Navy testified on May 8, 2013, that it is

> aggressively pursuing commonality between the two variants, with particular focus on weapon systems, sensors, and C4I equipment. There are several on-going studies that will identify non-recurring integration costs, insertion points, and total ownership costs in order to assess the optimal insertion points.[125]

Life-Cycle Operation and Support (O&S) Costs

Any savings the dual-award strategy might realize relative to the down select strategy in terms of costs for procuring LCSs could also be offset by potential additional life-cycle operation and support (O&S) costs of operating significant numbers of two different LCS designs. A December 8, 2010, GAO report states: "According to the Navy, [estimated savings in LCS procurement costs under the dual-award strategy] would be offset, in part, by an additional $842 million in total ownership costs, which the Navy equates to a net present value of $295 million."[126] The Navy confirmed this figure at the December 14 hearing, and stated that this estimate was carefully prepared and consistent with past Navy analyses on this question.

GAO's December 8 report states:

> Navy officials expressed confidence that their cost estimate supporting the dual award provides details on the costs to operate and support both designs. However, since little actual LCS operating and support data are available to date, the Navy's estimates for these costs are currently based on data from other ships and could change as actual cost data become more available. These estimates are also based on new operational concepts for personnel, training, and maintenance that have not been fully developed, tested, and implemented. For example, the Navy has not yet implemented a comprehensive training plan, and it is possible that the plan could cost more or less than the training costs currently accounted for by the Navy.[127]

---

[123] Mike McCarthy, "LCS-5, -6 Will Keep Separate Combat Systems, PEO Says," *Defense Daily*, August 18, 2011: 3-4.

[124] Christopher P. Cavas, "U.S. Navy Weighs Halving LCS Order," *DefenseNews.com*, March 17, 2013.

[125] Statement of The Honorable Sean J. Stackley, Assistant Secretary of the Navy (Research, Development and Acquisition) and Vice Admiral Allen G. Myers, Deputy Chief of Naval Operations for Integration of Capabilities and Resources and Vice Admiral Kevin M. McCoy, Commander, Naval Sea Systems Command, Before the Subcommittee on Seapower of the Senate Armed Services Committee on Department of the Navy Shipbuilding Programs, May 8, 2013, p. 13.

[126] Government Accountability Office, *Navy's Proposed Dual Award Acquisition Strategy for the Littoral Combat Ship Program*, GAO-11-249R, December 8, 2010, Table 1 on page 3.

[127] Government Accountability Office, *Navy's Proposed Dual Award Acquisition Strategy for the Littoral Combat Ship Program*, GAO-11-249R, December 8, 2010, p. 6.

CBO's December 10 letter report states:

> Operating and maintaining two types of ships would probably be more expensive, however. The Navy has stated that the differences in costs are small (and more than offset by procurement savings), but there is considerable uncertainty about how to estimate those differences because the Navy does not yet have much experience in operating such ships.[128]

Resulting Net Costs

Using the above information, it appears that the Navy estimates that, compared to the down select strategy, the dual award strategy might save a net total of $615 million (net present value) through FY2016, or $201 million (net present value) through FY2015. This figure includes $910 million (net present value) in savings in ship procurement costs through FY2016, or $496 million (net present value) in ship procurement costs through FY2015, less $295 million (net present value) in additional ship O&S costs.

This figure does not account for possible changes in the costs of other Navy ships that might be occur as a consequence of changes in the spreading of shipyard fixed overhead costs. The estimated net savings of $615 million (net present value) through FY2016 ($201 million [net present value] through FY2015) would be reduced by any LCS combat system modification costs. Navy testimony at the December 14 hearing suggests that combat system modification costs might range from zero (no modifications) to a few tens of millions of dollars (changing the radar on the ships).

Using CBO's estimate rather than the Navy's estimate for relative ship procurement costs (see **Table D-1**) would make the dual-award strategy more expensive than the down select strategy. As mentioned earlier, the Navy witnesses at the December 14 hearing defended the Navy's estimate of ship procurement costs, stating that it was based on actual bid data from the two LCS bidders, and that CBO's estimate did not reflect full exposure to these bid data, because the data are proprietary and being closely held by the Navy pending a potential announcement by the Navy of a down select decision (if the dual-award strategy is not pursued).

Relative Risks

Regarding the potential relative risks of the down select and dual-award acquisition strategies, the December 8 GAO report states that "a second ship design and source provided under the dual award strategy could provide the Navy an additional hedge against risk, should one design prove problematic."[129] It might also be argued that the dual-award strategy avoids the construction risks present under the down select strategy of having LCSs built by a shipyard that has not previously built LCSs.

On the other hand, it might be argued that if there *is* a substantial risk of an LCS design proving problematic, then the LCS program should not be put into series production in the first place, and that if there *is not* a substantial risk of an LCS design proving problematic, then the value of

---

[128] Congressional Budget Office, letter report to Senator John McCain on LCS acquisition strategies dated December 10, 2010, p. 3.

[129] Government Accountability Office, *Navy's Proposed Dual Award Acquisition Strategy for the Littoral Combat Ship Program*, GAO-11-249R, December 8, 2010, p. 4.

hedging against that risk would be negligible. It might also be argued that managing the construction of two very different LCS designs could place increased demands on overall Navy program management capacities and on the Navy's Supervisor of Shipbuilding (SUPSHIP) capabilities for on-site monitoring of the construction of Navy ships—factors that might increase the chances of program-management challenges in the LCS program or of the Navy not detecting in a timely manner construction-quality problems that might occur in one or both LCS designs.[130]

---

[130] Limits on Navy SUPSHIP capacities may have been a factor in the delayed discovery by the Navy of construction quality problems on Navy San Antonio (LPD-17) class amphibious ships. For a discussion of LPD-17 class construction quality problems, CRS Report RL34476, *Navy LPD-17 Amphibious Ship Procurement: Background, Issues, and Options for Congress*, by Ronald O'Rourke.

Appendix E. Additional Material Relating to Question of Whether to Truncate LCS Program

This appendix presents some additional reference material relating to the question of whether to truncate the LCS program.

July 2012 Press Report on Internal Navy Reviews of Program

Regarding the prospective ability of the LCS to perform missions, a July 14, 2012, press report based on some of the internal Navy reviews of the LCS program that led to the August 2012 establishment of the LCS Council states:

> The original idea for the littoral combat ship (LCS) envisioned modular mission packages that could be rapidly swapped, so one ship could change missions easily from mine warfare, for example, to anti-submarine warfare over the course of a single deployment.
>
> But instead of taking just days to make the switch, it's now apparent it could take weeks. An LCS assigned to a particular operation will likely operate in a single "come-as-you-are" configuration, requiring additional ships equipped with other mission modules to provide the flexibility the concept once promised.
>
> That's one conclusion among many following a series of Navy exercises and reports intended to take stock of LCS. Other conclusions criticize the ship as failing to match capabilities inherent to the ships it would replace. The assessment aims to figure out what the ship can and can't do, how it should be employed, what kind of support it will need, and what changes must be made to man and fight the ships without wearing out their small crews.
>
> These include a classified study ordered by Adm. Mark Ferguson, the vice chief of naval operations; two war games carried out by U.S. Fleet Forces Command (USFFC) in Norfolk, Va.; and the ongoing operating experiences of the two ships already in service....
>
> The classified study, known as the OPNAV report (referring to staff reporting to the chief of naval operations), was headed by Rear Adm. Samuel Perez. Beginning in January, Perez and a 10-person team looked at all aspects of the fleet's "readiness to receive, employ and deploy" the LCS.
>
> USFFC in January conducted a "sustainment war game" to understand the issues and risks in manning and supporting an LCS across the Pacific Ocean—a key concern with the Freedom, the first LCS, scheduled to deploy to Singapore in the spring of 2013. It will be the first time an LCS has operated outside the Western Hemisphere.
>
> Another war game, focusing on operations and war fighting, was held in mid-June. The results of that effort are still being analyzed, Navy sources said.
>
> While the Navy would not release the OPNAV report, a number of sources familiar with both LCS and the report said it lays out in greater detail the problems and issues confronting the entire LCS effort, including the concept of operations (CONOPS), manning shortages, maintenance and training concerns, modularity and mission module issues, and commonality problems between the two LCS variants.

It also cites problems with how the LCS is perceived in the fleet, how leadership presents LCS capabilities, and the need to effect changes in virtually every operational area.

"As I looked at some of the draft documentation to say how we're going to run LCS, what I thought we needed to do was a rebaselining, understanding how much information we've generated on how we're going to operate these ships, and take that and build a foundation," said Rear Adm. Thomas Rowden, OPNAV's director of surface warfare, during an interview at the Pentagon. "I will call this a concept of employment, or CONEMP."

Rowden is leading the work to coordinate and compile the LCS analytical efforts.

"The reality of it is, it's time to step back and say, what did we get wrong here?"

CONOPS

Planners originally envisaged the LCS as a replacement for the fleet's frigates, minesweepers and patrol boats, but the new assessments conclude the ships are not equal to today's frigates or mine countermeasures ships, and they are too large to operate as patrol boats.

The LCS, according to the assessments, is not able to fulfill most of the fleet missions required by the Navy's primary strategy document, the "Cooperative Strategy for 21st Century Seapower," and included in a 2011 revision of the LCS CONOPS document.

Equipped with a surface warfare or maritime security mission package, the ships were judged capable of carrying out theater security cooperation and deterrence missions, and maritime security operations, such as anti-piracy.

But the LCS vessels cannot successfully perform three other core missions envisioned for them—forward presence, sea control or power projection missions—and they can provide only limited humanitarian assistance or disaster relief operations, sources said.

The shortcomings are well known in the fleet, prompting a perception that service leaders are looking for missions to fit LCS, rather than the other way around.

A key LCS failure identified by the OPNAV report, sources said, is its inability to effectively defend against anti-ship cruise missiles (ASCMs), a weapon carried by hundreds of small, fast-attack craft operated by virtually all potentially hostile navies....

The U.S. Navy's requirements document for the LCS says it must be able to operate offensively in multithreat environments—areas that would include the Arabian Gulf or the Yellow Sea—but until a solution is found, the assessments call for a CONOPS more consistent with the ships' capabilities, and suggest the need for studies to increase LCS combat power.

The Navy is continuing to look at ways to increase the ship's weaponry and lethality. A major gap is for a weapon to replace the Non-Line of Sight Launch System (NLOS-LS), a surface-to-surface missile program canceled in 2010 that was to have given the LCS a prodigious capability.

"I certainly have asked to take a look at Harpoon, if we can take the weight," Rowden said. "Also looking at the Griffin," a small weapon being purchased for a trial installation on the Freedom. "There are some other missiles that we're looking at, but those are the two I can talk about right now."

The Harpoon is currently the Navy's standard surface-to-surface missile, carried on destroyers and cruisers. But adding such a missile would probably mean removing something else to compensate for the additional weight. The Griffin is much smaller, but doesn't pack the Harpoon's punch.

Rowden also has asked the Naval Sea Systems Command (NAVSEA) to study replacing the 57mm gun on both LCS designs with a 76mm weapon, similar to the weapon on today's frigates.

"It's a larger gun, more range, certainly gives us a better opportunity to engage the enemy," Rowden said of the 76mm.

The trouble with that weapon is that it can fit on Freedom LCS 1-class ships, but not on the narrow bow of the trimaran Independence LCS 2-class. "I don't know if we can get it on both hulls," Rowden acknowledged.

Range is still another concern, because of capacity for both fuel and crew provisions. Although the original CONOPS called for ships to operate at sea for at least 21 days, the ships have storage capacity to only carry enough food for 14 days, according to sources familiar with the classified report....

Eventually, all the effort will be gathered into the concept of employment, or CONEMP, document.

"It is not going to be a static document," Rowden declared. "We're going to be inputting things, and as we learn things we're going to make modifications to keep it relevant and reflect experience.

"We've got folks from Fleet Forces Command, Pacific Fleet, Naval Surface Forces, Naval Air Forces, NAVSEA, OPNAV and the manpower assessment team all working together to try and understand what we've observed and what we have learned so we can have a good, informed document with respect to this concept of employment," Rowden said.

"My gut tells me we've got to get the manning squared away, then the training, sustainment and maintenance will flow from that as we move forward," he added. "We'll get to a better place to say these are the things we need to do to maximize the availability and capability of the ships."[131]

An August 2, 2012, Navy information paper responding to the above article states:

1. ASSERTION: The Mission Package quick-swap concept is dead.

RESPONSE: Each LCS will deploy with the Mission Package (MP) required to accomplish the Combatant Commander (COCOM)-directed missions. As expected, if COCOMs direct a MP swap, materiel staging and personnel movement will need to be planned and coordinated in advance. The physical swap of MP equipment can occur in less than 96 hours, as the requirement dictates.

---

[131] Christopher P. Cavas, "LCS: Quick Swap Concept Dead," *DefenseNews.com*, July 14, 2012. See also Tony Capaccio, "Navy Ship Can't Meet Mission, Internal Report Finds," *Bloomberg News*, May 6, 2013; Christopher P. Cavas, "Maintenance Hurdles Mount for New USN Ship," *DefenseNews.com*, July 23, 2012; Michael Fabey, "U.S. Navy Finds More LCS-1 Issues During Special Trials," *Aerospace Daily & Defense Report*, June 21, 2012: 2; Christopher P. Cavas, "U.S. Navy's LCS Yet to Fulfill Its Promise," *DefenseNews.com*, April 15, 2012.

2. ASSERTION: Planners originally envisaged LCS as a replacement for Frigates, Minesweepers, and Patrol Boats, but new assessments conclude that the ships are not equal to the legacy ships.

RESPONSE: While LCS will provide the capabilities and conduct the missions currently performed by the FFG, MCM and PC type ships, LCS is not a direct class replacement for any of these. It is a new ship type with distinct capabilities. LCS with its mission packages will provide equal or greater capability than the legacy platforms whose missions it is assuming.

3. ASSERTION: LCS vessels cannot successfully perform three other core missions envisioned for them-forward presence, sea control or power projection.

RESPONSE: LCS will be able to perform all of the missions for which she was built. As the ships transition from research and development assets to operational Fleet units, the ongoing efforts to determine the infrastructure requirements and sustainment processes will be implemented and provide the requisite support to enable the successful execution of these missions.

4. ASSERTION: Key failure is inability to effectively defend against ASCMs.

RESPONSE: LCS, with its 3-D air search radar and highly effective Rolling Airframe Missile, is at least as capable against the cruise missile threat as the CIWS-equipped FFG 7 and significantly more capable that the Avenger class MCM and Cyclone Class PC, which have no self-defense anti-cruise missile capability. LCS capability against ASCMs has been demonstrated with two live firings of RAM from LCS against cruise missile targets, as well as multiple tracking exercises and simulated ASCM engagements within the developmental test window.

5. ASSERTION: CONOPS dictates ships operate at sea for 21 days but ship can only store food for 14 days.

RESPONSE: The LCS CDD gives a 14-day threshold and a 30-day objective for replenishment, which supports the expected 21-day underway cycles referenced in the CONOPS. The CDD, not the CONOPS, is the governing document for all LCS requirements. And as noted earlier, when operating within its normal speed range profile (<15 knots), LCS has comparable endurance to an FFG 7.

6. ASSERTION: Navy is looking at ways to increase ship's weaponry and lethality.

RESPONSE: Every Navy weapon, sensor, ship and aircraft system is continually being reviewed and evaluated against current and future operations and threats to determine the best mix of total combat power that can be brought to the fight. LCS is no exception to this ongoing process.

7. ASSERTION: Major gap is the replacement of the Non-Line of Sight Launch System (NLOS-LS).

RESPONSE: While the cancellation of NLOS was indeed a setback in bringing the surface-to-surface missile to LCS, the modular design of LCS allows the Navy to select another missile, without costly redesign. As an interim solution, the Griffin missile has already been selected for incorporation until an extended range missile can be competitively awarded.[132]

Executive Summary of Navy "Perez Report" on Program

In late July 2013, the Navy released to the press a declassified version of the executive summary of the assessment directed by Rear Admiral Samuel Perez (i.e., the "Perez report"). The declassified executive summary, as posted at the Internet site of a defense trade press outlet and including a passage on the third page that was blacked out by the Navy, is reprinted below:[133]

---

[132] Navy information paper dated August 2, 2012, provided by Navy Office of legislative Affairs to CRS and CBO on August 2, 2012.

[133] The declassified version of the executive summary reprinted here was posted at InsideDefense.com (subscription required) on July 24, 2013. The blacked out passage on the third page is as posted at InsideDefense.com.

Section 1 - Executive Summary

On 6 January 2012, Vice Chief of Naval Operations, directed RDML Samuel Perez to assess and review the Navy's readiness to receive, employ and deploy the Littoral Combat Ship (LCS) class vessel. Appendix 001 contains the tasking letter. This report provides the review of the Navy's LCS readiness.

1.1   Systemic Barriers

The systemic barriers in Section 3 of this report are those issues which present the most far-reaching impediments to successful employment and deployment of the LCS program. Within each issue area, barriers may have both short- and long-range impacts on the ability to successfully execute the LCS program. Each must also be viewed as part of a composite picture of "LCS Wholeness," as the findings in one area usually have implications and effects across the rest of the spectrum.

1.2   Singular Barriers

The singular barriers in Section 4 of this report are divided across the DOTMLPF (doctrine, organization, training, maintenance, leadership, personnel, and facilities) spectrum. Each issue must again be viewed as part of a composite picture of "LCS Wholeness," with implications for the other issue areas. While these concerns will not typically have as wide-ranging an impact as the systemic barriers, the Navy must mitigate them to successfully sustain the full 55-seaframe LCS program.

1.3   Overview

In order to determine barriers to LCS' introduction into the fleet, we started by reviewing key LCS tenets. Our review found that many people involved with the LCS program have forgotten key LCS fundamentals. Many have forgotten that the initial two hulls represent significant departures from the normal shipbuilding path; in fact, the focus of the first two ships is to refine concept development, modularity, employment of off-board vehicles and conduct risk mitigation for follow-on flights in the ship class. In essence designers viewed the first two ships as test and evaluation platforms. Innovative from its inception, the LCS program bypassed many of the traditional shipbuilding timelines by taking advantage of available commercial designs. The acquisition strategy sought to quickly produce a seaframe—the hull without the associated combat systems package—and deploy it to the fleet for Sailor experimentation. The goal was to quickly produce a high-speed, modular-mission ship designed to operate in the littorals in support of U.S. maritime objectives. Designers envisioned a fast, shallow-draft ship ideally suited for operations within constrained littoral environments. These characteristics would also enable LCS to forward deploy and engage a broader range of partners than possible with traditional cruiser/destroyer (CRUDES) ships.

Another innovative concept envisioned for LCS was "modularity." With modularity, the Navy designed an ability to exchange the ship's main battery, mission packages (MPs). Each of the MPs would bring a unique capability to the ship. The versatile surface warfare (SUW) MP would be designed for routine littoral operations. The mine countermeasures (MCM) MP would use off-board sensors and vehicles to deliver a mine warfare capability. In the same manner, the

1

anti-submarine warfare (ASW) MP would employ sensors and helicopters to find and prosecute quiet diesel submarines in the littorals.

Interviews with early LCS designers and requirements officers confirmed that the Navy did not intend LCS to assume the role of a small multi-mission frigate or a "pocket" DDG. Instead, LCS would operate in conjunction with more capable ships in a netted environment providing integrated air and missile-defense. On-board systems would provide LCS with an adequate self-defense capability for most littoral environments. In addition, speed would enable LCS to press the fight when capable and withdraw when required. Embarked aviation assets would broaden LCS' surveillance envelope and provide the ship with an alternate means of expanding the battlespace.

Few innovative concepts are perfect from the start. LCS is no exception. Our review revealed seven areas that require closer alignment with the CNO's Tenets to effectively integrate LCS into fleet operations: the concept of operations, manning, maintenance, modularity, MP capability, training, and commonality.

The first step in "getting LCS right" is to determine the correct concept of operations (CONOPS). The Navy advertises LCS as a replacement for three ship classes: frigates (FFGs), mine countermeasure ships (MCMs), and patrol craft (PCs). Designers believed that LCS' modularity would enable it to adequately perform missions across the wide spectrum of operations performed by the three ship classes. The Navy drafted the initial CONOPS accordingly. This review highlights the gap between ship capabilities and the missions the Navy will need LCS to execute.

There are two options: building a CONOPS to match LCS' current capabilities or modifying the ship to better meet the needs of the Theater Commanders. As stated previously, LCS is not a smaller frigate, but neither was it intended to be solely a patrol boat. In its current design, LCS provides the Theater Commander with focused capabilities in the littorals. It is an ideal partnership asset that can increase U.S. presence in many areas previously inaccessible to our Navy. Planners must take care to assign LCS to appropriate operational areas and missions that closely match the ships' capabilities. The ships' current characteristics limit operations to a greater extent than envisioned by the CONOPS and ROC/POE developers. As configured, LCS' characteristics require the ship to pull into port more frequently to replenish, provide crew rest, and conduct maintenance.

The second option is to modify the ship to support the warfighting requirements. Our review identified opportunities to modify several of the ships' characteristics to more closely align with the intent of the original CONOPS. These modifications also enable LCS to more fully assume the operational roles of the three ship classes.

The current manning construct does not provide enough depth to execute the CONOPS, meet ROC/POE requirements, or support LCS' forward operational concept. At present, LCS manning sacrifices the ships' operational capabilities and systems reliability, and requires senior, qualified Sailors in numbers that many view as unsupportable. The contract maintenance scheme, primarily driven by the low number of assigned Sailors, is inadequate to maintain required systems and seaframe availability, and may place too many operational limits on forward-deployed units.

2

Originally, designers envisioned modularity as a method to quickly swap-out MPs, providing the ship with a tactical means of shifting from one focused mission to another. Logistics realities, especially those associated with forward-deployed naval forces, indicate that the timeline for an MP exchange will depend largely on in-theater logistics resources and capabilities. The logistics and training challenges tied to conducting MP change-outs leads most operational commanders to predict that ships will retain their embarked MPs for extended periods of time. Modularity remains a highly desirable capability; however, the decision to exchange MPs will more likely be an operational rather than a tactical decision. Given the challenges and timelines associated with an MP change-out, all stakeholders must understand modularity's current limitations.

Meanwhile, the current capabilities delivered by two of the three MPs fall short of the requirements needed to satisfy the CONOPS. The ASW MP comes late. The MCM MP is behind schedule and must overcome a few remaining challenges, but is nearing fleet introduction.

The LCS minimal-manning construct also requires Sailors to be highly trained before they arrive on the ship. In contrast to the approach used aboard most ships, each Sailor qualifies on their watchstation prior to reporting aboard (Train to Qualify – T2Q). Taking training beyond the apprentice-to-journeyman construct found in the fleet, LCS Sailors arrive with journeyman-level skills and integrate as a team, completing their certifications (Train to Certify – T2C) before reporting "on hull" as an integrated unit. Using this construct, the entire crew arrives aboard the ship as a full up round. The requirement to deliver qualified Sailors drives a lengthy training pipeline, in many cases between 18 and 24 months of training before reporting to the ship or team.

Finally, with a view to future ship construction, divergent seaframes and ship systems prevent greater use of economies of scale for equipment, maintenance, and training. Driving to increased commonality will lower costs and increase flexibility in assigning LCS Sailors, who in many cases are not interoperable between variants.

Taking an innovative and forward leaning approach toward the maritime challenges of the future, LCS has the potential to be a remarkable ship and modularity an outstanding asset. However, to meet the CNO's Tenets of "Warfighting First, Operate Forward, and Be Ready," LCS must address the first six of the aforementioned issues as soon as practical. While not a barrier to initial operations, increasing LCS commonality will: yield economies of scale, increase LCS Sailor interoperability, simplify logistics, and enhance flexibility for operational commanders. Increasing commonality is crucial to creating a more cost-effective and sustainable ship over its lifetime.

3

June 2013 Navy Blog Post

A June 10, 2013, blog post on the LCS program from Rear Admiral John F. Kirby, the Chief of Information for the Navy, states:

> I've been following closely all the debate over the Littoral Combat Ship. I've even chimed in here and there to refute what I thought was bad reporting and erroneous claims by those using old information. I figure that's part of my job as the Navy's spokesman—not to staunchly defend but rather to inform and to educate.
>
> The truth is, these are healthy debates. We need them. Talking about problems is a good thing. And yet, as a guy who also taught naval history at the Academy, I can't help but think how very often we've been here before. Throughout our history, it seems, the boldest ideas are often the hardest to accept.
>
> Take legendary shipbuilder Joshua Humphreys, contracted in 1794 to build a new class of frigate for the fledgling American Navy. Longer and broader than traditional frigates, Humphrey's ships were designed with graceful underwater lines for speed, packing an impressive 44 guns and over an acre of sail.
>
> But to many, the design seemed freakish. With its angled hull curving inward from the waterline, unusually flush decks and several feet of extra beam, it was deemed too ungainly to be of service.
>
> Worse yet, Humphrey's design had only partial support from a reluctant Congress not particularly interested in stirring up the ire of the British or French, both of whom were at each other's throats again. We didn't need a Navy, not now, they said. And even if we did, it shouldn't consist of anything quite as drastic as Humphrey's frigates.
>
> All that changed in 1797, when, in response to warming relations between the United States and Great Britain, French privateers began raiding American commerce. By the summer of that year, they had captured no less than 300 U.S. ships.
>
> In a huff and in a hurry, Congress ordered the completion of three of Humphrey's frigates: United States, Constitution and Constellation.
>
> They would accord themselves well, proving vastly superior in speed and durability to their French foes. In one of the most famous battles of that short, little undeclared war, Constellation forced the surrender of one of France's mightiest frigates, Insurgente, in little more than an hour. Humphrey's frigates would go on to even greater glory against the Barbary pirates of the North African coast a few short years later.
>
> The critics had been silenced.
>
> Silencing critics became almost sport for a whole generation of ship designers and engineers in the early 1800s. Robert Fulton shut them up by proving the power of steam over wind; Commander John Dahlgren did it with a revolutionary new gun capable of far greater range and accuracy, and Swedish designer John Ericcson awed them with something called a gun turret.
>
> Ericcson didn't stop there, of course. He went on to design a whole new class of warship. He called them Monitors, and they changed naval warfare forever.

The Monitor's case is instructive for any discussion of LCS. Nearly everything about it was new and untried. Its features were striking: a long, low stealthy profile, making it hard to locate; a shallow draft and good maneuverability, making it perfect for work in the littorals; and a radically new weapons system that boasted the largest and most powerful gun in the Navy's inventory—John Dahlgren's.

The ship operated with less than a third the number of Sailors required of conventional warships. And it was multi-mission in scope, capable of offshore operations and supporting campaigns on land. Even the material used to form the hull—iron—was revolutionary and added to the ship's defensive capability.

Ericcson called it his "self-propelled battery at sea."

Critics called it a mistake. Too small, too slow and too lightly armed it would, they argued, be no match for the larger, cannon-bristling sloops of the Confederate Navy. Even Union Sailors had taken to calling it a "cheesebox on a raft."

It wasn't until much later in the war, after improvements had been made to the design, that the Monitor-class would prove its worth.

There were Monitors with Farragut at Mobile Bay. They took part in the Red River campaigns of the West and proved ideal for coastal blockading work. A Monitor even served as then-Admiral Dahlgren's flagship during the 1863 attack on Charleston. They proved durable ships and had an incredibly long service life, the last of them not being stricken from Navy rolls until 1937.

The spirit of Monitor—and every other type of revolutionary ship—is alive and well in LCS. As Monitor ushered in the era of armored ships and sounded the death knell for those of wood, so too will LCS usher in an era of a netted, flexible and modular capabilities.

With its interchangeable mission packages, its raw speed, and its ability to operate with so many other smaller navies around the world, LCS gives us a geo-strategic advantage we simply haven't enjoyed since the beginnings of the Cold War.

The response by Singapore and by other Pacific partners to Freedom's deployment, for example, has been overwhelmingly positive. They like the ship precisely because it isn't big, heavily-armed or overtly offensive. They like it because they can work with it. I fail to see how that's a bad thing in today's maritime environment.

Let's be honest. LCS was never intended to take on another fleet all by its own, and nobody ever expected it to bristle with weaponry. LCS was built to counter submarines, small surface attack craft, and mines in coastal areas. Thanks to its size and shallow draft, it can also conduct intelligence, surveillance, and reconnaissance operations, maritime security and intercept operations, as well as homeland defense missions. It can support Marines ashore, insert special operations forces and hunt down pirates in places we can't go right now.

Let me say that again … in places we can't go right now.

That counts for something. The CNO always talks about building a Navy that can be where it matters and ready when it matters. Well, the littorals matter. The littorals are where products come to market; it's where seaborne trade originates. Littorals include the major straits, canals, and other maritime chokepoints so necessary to this traffic. It's also where a whole lot of people live. Coastal cities are home to more than three billion people right now, a figure that some experts estimate will double by 2025.

In addition to strains on local economies and the environment, this rapid population growth will continue to exacerbate political, social, cultural and religious tensions. You don't have to look any further than today's headlines to see the truth in that. Consider the Levant, North Africa, the South China Seas. And you don't have to look any further than at our current fleet of ships to see what we're missing.

We need this ship. We also need to be more clear about it—what it is and what it isn't. This ship is a light frigate, a corvette. I never understood why we didn't just call it that in the first place. Maybe it's because a corvette conveys something less muscular, less macho. I don't know. Maybe it's because a corvette is something completely new to us, at least those of us with no memories of picket destroyers, PT-boats, and hydrofoils.

Remember the whole debate over the Perry-class frigates? I sure do. My first ship was a frigate. Too small, the critics said, too slow, too vulnerable. It couldn't defend itself, they argued. The 76mm gun was little more than a pea-shooter. The Phalanx system, poorly situated aft on the O-2 level, fired rounds too small to be effective against incoming missiles. The sonar? Well, let's just say that some people compared it being both deaf and blind. Sailors on cruisers and destroyers used to joke that "they wished they were on a 'fig' so they could get sub pay."

As one contemporary observer noted, "When [then] Soviet Admiral of the Fleet Sergei Gorshkov goes to bed at night, he's not lying awake counting Oliver Hazard Perry frigates."

And yet, the little frigates became one of the most useful—and most popular—ships in the Navy. "By saving money, manpower, and operating costs, the FFGs helped the Navy pass through the economic trough of the 1970s and, with upgrades available from increased defense spending in the 1980s, have served as a reliable platform through the end of the 20th century," writes Dr. Timothy L. Francis, a naval historian.

"Moreover," he continues, "without these low-end ships the U.S. Navy never would have been able to grow to the numbers needed to conduct the last phase of the Cold War, which allowed the service to meet the multi-faceted challenges of that period."

Criticism is good. Criticism is healthy. We should have to justify to the very public we are charged to protect how we are spending their hard-earned tax dollars. And we are. We're working very hard to be as forthright and open as we can about all the problems still plaguing both variants of the ship. But let's not forget that it was critics who laughed at the aircraft carrier, disparaged the F/A-18 Hornet and the MV-22, and scoffed at the idea of propelling submarine through the water with the power locked inside an atom.

The critics have been plenty wrong before. And even the most skeptical of us have to be willing to admit that they will be wrong again.

Look, LCS isn't perfect—by any stretch. But it's still experimental. It's still a bit like Humphrey's Constellation and Ericcson's Monitor when they first joined the fleet. New and untried, yes, but valuable in their own way to making us a more capable Navy. It just takes a little time to prove the concept. Sailors didn't exactly clamor for PT-boat duty in World War II until it became a tactically proven and exciting option for them.

Navy leaders have been very clear that all options for LCS remain on the table. If we find that LCS needs to be more lethal, we'll make it more lethal. If we find the ship needs to be manned or maintained differently, we'll do that too. Just like with the Perry-class, we'll upgrade and we'll update. We'll change.

But one thing that hasn't changed is the dangerous world we live in. The threats and the opportunities we face are real. And, quite frankly, they are every bit as "multi-faceted" as were those we faced at the end of the Cold War.

As Aviation Week's Mike Fabey wrote recently, "The Navy needs to rid the service of the 'old think.'"

"Whether the Navy achieves operational or acquisition success with LCS remains to be seen," he noted. "But we do most definitely have a ship that is designed to be operated far differently than any other warship before it. At the high-altitude conceptual level, that is precisely what the Navy wanted."

He's absolutely right. We want—and we need—a new class of ships that can meet these new challenges, that can get us on station fast and close, one that can perform in the coastal areas where our partners, our forces and our potential foes will also operate.

To the critics I say, this is such a ship. Give it time.[134]

Author Contact Information

Ronald O'Rourke
Specialist in Naval Affairs
rorourke@crs.loc.gov, 7-7610

---

[134] John F. Kirby, "The Littoral Combat Ship: Give It Time," *InformationDissemination.net*, June 10, 2013, accessed July 2, 2013, at http://www.informationdissemination net/2013/06/the-littoral-combat-ship-give-it-time.html. Ellipsis as in original. For another blog post by a Navy admiral in defense of the LCS (in this case, by Rear Admiral Thomas S. Rowden, the Navy's Director of Surface Warfare), see Thomas S. Rowden, "Littoral Combat Ships: The Value of Forward Presence and Numbers," Navy Live, May 24, 2013, accessed July 2, 20131, at http://navylive.dodlive mil/2013/05/24/littoral-combat-ships-the-value-of-forward-presence-and-numbers/.